About the Author

"All-American in Plaster" — a newspaper article gave Dan Clark this nickname because of his numerous injuries that cut short his dreams of a professional athletic career. Dan broke his neck twice and fractured two vertebrae, his nose, left arm, both thumbs, hands, and little fingers. He tore both knees three times and both ankles twice, and has had surgery for appendicitis, two hernias, and a torn knee. He also has been sewn up eleven times on his head, shoulder, and hand.

However, through it all, Dan has become an authority on self belief and motivation skills and has evolved into a sensitive, courageous, and successful young man. As president of his own training and consulting corporation, he is a full-time professional speaker, addressing more than 200,000 students, advisors, and business people from coast to coast each year. Dan was sponsored by the world-renowned Mr. Zig Ziglar, as a member of the prestigious National Speakers Association; he is also a speaker with the Leadership Development Institute of Oklahoma City, an Executive Speaker with the Chamber of Commerce Speakers Bureau, and a member of Toastmasters International.

In high school, Dan twice was voted outstanding class athlete, lettering eight times in football, basketball, baseball, and track. He received a full-football scholarship and chose to attend the University of Utah where he majored in English. As an outstanding defensive end, a professional contract seemed automatic until a paralyzing nerve injury cut short his football career. However, Dan didn't give up, and he has an amazing rehabilitation story to tell!

Dan has always enjoyed "getting high," as his experiences range from motorcycle racer, ski racer, amateur boxer, musician, and television actor to judge of the Miss Utah Beauty Pageant. He is the writer and recording artist of an album of songs, author of two books, and producer of a popular cassette tape, video, and film series.

In recognition of his many accomplishments and service to his fellowmen, Dan was named an Outstanding Young Man of America in 1982.

"A child is a person who is going to carry on what you have started. He is going to sit where you are sitting, and when you are gone, attend to those things which you think are important. You may adopt all the policies you please, but how they are carried out depends on him. He will assume control of your cities, states, and nation. He is going to move in and take over your churches, schools, universities, and corporations. . . . the fate of humanity is in his hands."

— Abraham Lincoln

"If one advances confidently in the directions of his dreams and endeavors to live the life which he has imagined, he will meet with a success unimagined in common hours."

— Henry David Thoreau

GETTING HIGH

HOW TO <u>REALLY</u> DO IT

BY DAN CLARK

Illustrated by Barbara Sansom

Published by
KARRINGTON COMPANY
1983

Lithographed in the United States of America by Publishers Press

Published by
KARRINGTON COMPANY
1983

Contents

Introduction

Books are read for many reasons: for entertainment, to overcome boredom, to acquire knowledge, to increase understanding. Why are you reading this one?

Is it because you know or have met the author? Does the title intrigue you? Did a teacher or counselor at school recommend it? If so, these are good reasons, but they are not good enough. *Getting High* is a self-help book and unless you are reading it because you really want to help yourself and become better today than you were yesterday, the contents will do you no good.

Life presents many ups and downs with accompanying emotional highs and lows. And as you analyze your experiences in life, I'm sure you'll agree that most of your successes in life have come when you were feeling high, when you were on the upswing. They occurred when you were excited and motivated to do your best. They happened because you knew who you were, liked what you were doing, and had a proper mental attitude.

Sure, attitude alone didn't bring you success, but then neither did knowledge and ability by themselves make you a winner.

Motivation without planned direction causes frustration. Therefore, to be successful, a person must possess, understand, and apply a combination of both motivation and planned direction. That's why I wrote this book. *Getting High* is more than emotional peppery. It's not just a psychological shot in the arm. *Getting High* is a mental meal. It's a "how-to" book that takes you from

7

"hello" to "good-bye" on the reasons for and the steps to getting your body, mind, and life in condition to achieve. And the message doesn't end when the cover shuts or the reading light clicks off. In fact, that is when the real learning begins. The enthusiasm, dreams, ambitions, and attitudes of youth — that's what this book is all about.

I realize many motivational books have already been written. But I also realize that corporations, salespeople, and parents have been the target audiences. That's why this book is unique, effective, and important. Even though all ages can benefit, it is written especially for tomorrow's leaders — today's youth.

Youth are tomorrow's leaders. Youth are the hope and backbone of the future. Youth are inventors, lawyers, agriculturists, educators, laborers, doctors, presidents, world record holders — all in embryo. Youth have the raw, naked ability to do the impossible! All they need is direction, encouragement, and the right kind of motivation.

As you read this book, keep in mind that you were born to succeed, and program yourself in the spirit of Pericles' counsel to ancient Athens: ". . . contemplate Athens not alone for what she is, but for what she has the power to become."

Realize that the power to become is found in living where you are — right now — in present time. When you can acknowledge all the things you are afraid you are, and all the things you are pretending to be, the only thing left is the present you. And working on the present you is the purpose of this book. Therefore, as you begin, set your goals high to "get high," prepare to laugh at yourself, and remember, "the best is yet to be"!

Chapter One

"Getting High"

How to Really Do It

Let's face it. "Getting high" is the only way we have to cope with life. In fact, getting high is the most important thing you can learn to do right now; it is the solution to all of your challenges in life. You need to get high to like yourself, to get along with your parents, and to effectively communicate with your friends.

Interested in using what I've got? You should be because the "high" I'm referring to is much better than "Black Velvet," "Kona Gold," or the best "Dust" in town. And getting high my way requires no money, chemicals, or preservatives.

You see, my high is the natural high that anyone can get from life. It's true! It's a scientifically, medically, humanly proven fact that you can "catch a buzz" from life. According to Norman Cousins, getting high is a sensation that occurs naturally as we laugh, cry, exude extra effort, or endure extreme pain. When we engage in any one of the above, our brain manufactures a substance called endorphin that acts on our system as a natural stimulant and pain killer. It is similar to morphine (notice the spelling likeness) in that it gives us a feeling of excitement or relief when our activity warrants it. It is also addictive in a sense, as is morphine, in that once we experience this

9

natural high a number of times, our system continues to crave whatever can make us feel that way again. Hence the long-distance runner who continually pushes his body beyond its pain barrier and constantly uses endorphin to do so becomes "addicted" to running.

Is getting high on life easy to do? You bet it is! As I indicated, one way to get endorphin to flow freely is through laughter. And the source doesn't always come in the form of a great joke. It's mostly found in everyday life. All you have to do is look for it.

For example, I remember overhearing a conversation between my high school principal and a boy who wanted to be on the school debate team. After the tryouts were over, the principal stopped the student in the hall and asked, "Did you make the debate team?"

"No," he disappointedly answered, "Th-They s-s-said I w-wasn't t-t-tall enough!"

I recall another humorous time when we had a school boxing tournament to raise charity money and my buddy Tony decided to participate. After a disastrous first round, my friends and I went over to Tony's corner to see what was happening. I thought I would die laughing when I heard the conversation between Tony and his trainer.

Tony asked, "Have I done any damage?"

His trainer answered, "No, but keep swinging. Maybe the draft will give him a cold!"

Thinking back to high school always reminds me of my first kiss, and how I tried to figure out the technique to get another one. Practical application of mathematics seemed a good way to accomplish this goal and this poem from David Mickel's book, *Dating and Other Frightening Experiences*, explains what happened.

> He's teaching her arithmetic, he said it was his mission,
> He kissed her once, he kissed her twice, and said, "Now that's addition."
> And as he added smack by smack in silent satisfaction,
> She sweetly gave the kisses back and said, "Now that's subtraction."
> Then he kissed her, she kissed him without an explanation.
> Then both together smiled and said, "That's multiplication."
> Then Dad appeared upon the scene and made a quick decision,
> He kicked that kid three blocks away and said, "That's long division."

11

Productive Highs

"Laughter highs" are not the only kind of highs we can experience. "Productive highs" also provide a stimulating sensation and occur when our adrenalin starts to flow.

For example, when I was in college, I had a special opportunity to take some time off from playing football to further my education without losing any eligibility. During this time, I got so caught up in what I was doing that I couldn't find time to work out and stay in shape. Therefore, when I returned to football, I looked like the "Pillsbury Dough Boy." I was so out of shape that I was embarrassed to go in the weight room when any of the other players were around. So each day I sneaked in early to work out with my brother Paul to catch up to the average strength of the rest of the team before anyone knew the difference. I had only been back two weeks when it was announced that we had a team "max" day — a test day when we lift as much weight as we can in front of the coaches for a grade. I thought, How could they do this to me when I still look like Herbert Milktoast? They'll think I'm a pencil-neck for sure! At this point in time my "max" on the bench press was only 225 pounds pushed one time. What a joke! No matter how hard I tried, I could not lift more than 225 pounds, once.

The "max" day came for us to be tested. But instead of just the coaches being there, the whole team showed up! I was now on the spot! My turn came up on the bench press and the coach asked me how much weight I wanted to warm up with before my "max" lift. Trying to be cool I said, "Oh, it doesn't matter — whatever." To this, the coach had the guys put on 225 pounds and asked, "Is this enough?" I about dropped my knickers! Who was he fooling? I couldn't warm up with that much weight even if I ran a forty-yard sprint at it and used my legs, feet, and head to lift it. The coach was serious, though, and I couldn't let on that I was a weakling, so I went ahead with it.

Looking in the mirror on the wall for some inner strength, I tried to get psyched up. I was hoping to see Lou Ferrigno (the Incredible Hulk) staring at me saying, "You can do it," but instead, there I was — Don Knotts, winking and saying, "You couldn't beat your way out of a wet paper bag." I made Gomer Pyle look like Mr. Universe!

So I stalled as long as I could, took a deep breath, sat down on the bench, positioned my hands on the bar, and went for it.

And you know what happened? I did it! In fact, I pressed it ten times, quickly and with ease! And when I got off, I looked at the coach and said, "Yea, it was nothing! I guess I should have used more weight!" (Ha! Ha!) I was so high I almost floated out of the room. I had not been able to lift this much weight since I had returned home. But I defied the odds, overcame intimidation, and succeeded when even *I* didn't give me a prayer.

Service Highs

Another kind of high I experienced that definitely ranks at the top of my list comes from love and service to our fellowmen — a "service high." Although I didn't perform the service I'm about to relate, I was lucky enough to experience it vicariously. This heart-warming story makes true the statement, "Some people are crippled by adversity, some are destroyed by it, others are made by it."

It took place in 1968 at the University of Utah football stadium, the site of the annual state Special Olympics track and field meet — a competition held especially for mentally and physically handicapped individuals.

One participant, a motor-handicapped, brain-damaged young man who could walk but definitely could not run, is the center of this tender story. His name is Kim Peek. Every time I think about it, I get choked up and watered down with tears.

Kim was racing in a fifty-yard dash against two other kids, severe cerebral palsy victims, who were in wheelchairs. When the gun went off, Kim started "running" for victory. One of the two other participants kept running into the wall and turning her wheelchair around while the other, who was turned backwards so he could push the wheelchair with his feet, was also struggling. Ahead by twenty yards and only ten yards from the finish line, Kim turned around to see how the others were coming. Seeing the difficulty they were having, Kim stopped and went back to help push the little girl who was against the wall across the line. In the meantime, the boy going backwards won the race. And because Kim was pushing the wheelchair, the girl took second and he came in last. Kim, however, did win the sportsmanship medal which he proudly has hanging on his wall at home.

Take One More Step

You see, getting high in life, on life, and from life is essential and easy! But it's not automatic. Laughing, giving extra effort, serving, enduring pain — it all takes a constant effort.

The other day I was shopping in a large department store when I saw life demonstrated in its most basic form. A mother with three children came down an escalator and began walking through the store. However, her youngest son was not paying attention and thought the family was going down to another floor. Therefore, he hopped on the next escalator and was halfway down before his mother noticed. In a loud scream the mother shouted, "Billy, no! Come back here right now!" To this, the startled child turned and started to run back up the down-moving escalator. After about two minutes of hard, determined, sweaty sprinting, and despite the fact that his mother, brothers, and several store customers were cheering him on, the tired little boy decided he needed a rest. What a heartbreaking scene! He was just three steps away from the top when he stopped and the escalator took him all the way back to the bottom where he had to start over again.

Life is exactly the same way. We are riding a down-moving escalator and each of us is struggling, through hard work and determination, to climb against the movement. And the minute we feel we need a rest or feel we want to relax and kick back for a while, opportunities of life pass us by and we are taken back to the point where we began.

This analogy can also be applied to getting high on life. Getting high is not a destination; it's a journey, a continuous process. All that is required is that you willingly take one more step. And anyone can do that!

I had the opportunity to be an assistant football coach at my old high school for the first few games of the 1982 season. During one particular practice, I observed the validity of this "one more step" principle in a practical, real-life situation.

Practice was over and it was time for me to run the players through conditioning. I decided to have them run ten fifty-yard windsprints. By the sixth one, over half of the team was starting to "dog" it, slow up, and complain about their fatigue. By the ninth sprint, most of the players were so tired that they were jogging. But do you know what happened as soon as I said, "One more"? The captains stepped forward and started to get the others psyched up. Soon the whole team joined in, and out of nowhere, each man found renewed energy and strength. When I finally blew the whistle, every man ran the tenth sprint harder than he ran the first. See! Anyone, regardless of where he or she is in life's game (tired, poor, hungry, uneducated, rich, powerful, famous) can take "one more step." Anyone can get psyched long enough to do something one more time! Therefore, getting high and reaching success doesn't necessarily come to the smartest individual, nor does it come to the one with the greatest number of talents and abilities. It comes to anyone and everyone who is willing to endure to the end and take that one more step. Reaching success is simple when you understand it.

If you haven't been high recently or haven't felt successful for a while, remember that it's not because you can't. It's because you don't understand. Here is the key: getting high comes as you constantly strive to understand your life, your opportunities, your associates, and yourself.

Understanding

A store owner was tacking on his window a sign which read, "Puppies for Sale." Signs like that have a way of attracting small children, and sure enough, a young boy appeared at the store owner's side. "How much are you going to sell the puppies for?" he asked.

The store owner explained, "These are very good dogs, and I don't expect to sell any of them for less than thirty-five dollars."

The little boy reached in his pocket, pulled out some change, quickly counted it, and said, "I have two dollars and thirty-seven cents. Can I look at 'em?"

The store owner smiled and whistled, and out of the kennel came Lady running down the aisle, followed by four little tiny balls of fur, one of which was lagging considerably behind.

Immediately the young boy singled out the limping, lagging puppy and inquired, "What's wrong with that one?"

The store owner explained that he had taken the puppy to the veterinarian and that the vet had said the puppy didn't have a hip socket and would always be lame.

In reply, the boy pointed at it again and said, "That's the puppy I want. I'll give you this money now and fifty cents a month until I get him paid for."

The store owner countered, "That would be fine, but you don't want that puppy. He'll never be able to run and jump and play with you like the other little dogs."

In response the little boy rolled up his right pant leg to reveal a badly twisted, crippled leg, supported by two steel braces, one running down each side, with a leather strap over his instep. "Well, sir," he confessed, "I don't run so well myself, and he'll need someone who understands."

Because the key to getting high on life is understanding, an appropriate conclusion to this chapter lies in the understanding that getting high is totally up to you. As you reflect on your past highs, I'm sure you'll agree they came when you were seeking for greatness; when you were working to become a champion, associating with winners, and stretching for success. Therefore, if you haven't felt high lately, you can change that! Don't let others influence you negatively or get you down. You take control — get yourself high again by attempting things that will push you to excellence. It's totally up to you, as is made clear in a paraphrased analogy by Dr. Maxwell Maltz.

Our bodies have built-in thermostats which maintain our inner physical temperature at a steady 98.6 degrees.

The outdoor weather may be cold or hot, but because our bodies do not take on the climate of our environment, they are able to maintain their own climate — a steady 98.6.

We also have within our minds an emotional "thermostat" that controls our highs and lows. It, like our body thermostat, also allows us to maintain a steady emotional climate in spite of the emotional weather around us. Therefore, we can get high and stay high whenever we choose! It's totally up to us and the situations we put ourselves into. All we need to do is raise our dreams and expectations, broaden our horizons, and adjust our emotional thermostats to "high." Getting high will then be constant and expected instead of occasional and accidental, and our lives will be everything we want them to be. It's true! Life is exactly as you perceive it. So if you want to be happy, if you want to get high, it's up to you to look on the bright side of everything.

A young boy who looked on the bright side of everything was given a ball and a bat by his father and told that when he got home from work, the father would play a whole inning of baseball with his son. Sure enough, when the father came home, he took his son out in the backyard to see what he could do.

The little boy threw the ball up, swung the bat, and missed. His father said, "Strike one."

The boy threw the ball up again, swung, and missed. His father said, "Strike two."

And with more determination than ever, the boy threw the ball up a third time, swung a mighty swing, missed, and spun around, falling to the grass. His father said, "Strike three, you're out. What do you think?"

To this, the positive-thinking, optimistic little boy answered, "Man, am I a good pitcher!"

Change your outlook from negative to positive; from average to above average; from ordinary to extraordinary. Think like Lance Allworth, the retired professional NFL receiver thinks. In high school Lance won fifteen letters in all sports, was drafted by the New York Yankees as a shortstop, was all-state in football, and went on to be a three-time Academic All-American in college. Lance says, "I had a good, easy childhood. I never wanted for anything.

But I've always loved football and taken pride in myself, and I have always forced myself to work hard enough to stay ahead of guys who were better than I was. I didn't have to work so hard. I could have kicked back and still been good — but not good enough."

This is the type of commitment you need to make to yourself as you proceed down the path to perfection. Be willing to make this commitment today. A man on a train who is debating whether to get off at the next stop cannot answer that question by delaying. To delay or postpone a decision is to actually make the decision. So it is with life. To put off is to actually make a decision — a negative one against doing. Life is made up of "one-way-or-the-other" events. Life does not postpone itself; it does not wait. Therefore, failure to act, and act *now*, is to miss opportunities for self-progression.

Keep this foremost in your mind as you continue to read through the exciting principles taught in this book. Commit now and reset your thermostat to "high"; realize that everything is possible to those who believe; believe that everyone was born to succeed; and remember that every day you can get as high as you like, on life!

Chapter Two

"Take Yourself Off the Shelf"

How to Get Started

There are literally thousands of schools in America that can teach you everything from accounting to zoology. They are efficient and effective at teaching facts and figures, and they graduate many who have much technical expertise.

But is this all that's necessary to succeed in life? Are knowledge and working skills the only ingredients in the recipe of success?

The answer can be demonstrated in the world of sports. For example, for every twenty thousand individuals participating in men's intercollegiate basketball, only one ever makes it to play on a professional team in the NBA. And in the NBA, only one out of every five players ever achieves the status of a "big name" star. Similar percentages hold true in all professional sports, as the combined total number of pro athletes adds up to only two thousand. Yet gyms and neighborhood lots all across the country are jammed with players who have enough ability and technical expertise to succeed in professional sports. Why, then, don't they? Obviously something more than ability and working skill plays an important part in success — not only in athletic success, but also in all areas and interests of everyday life.

Attitude, Not Scholarship, Determines Our Success

What is this missing ingredient? According to Zig Ziglar who quotes a Harvard University study, research shows that 85 percent of our success and accomplishments come as a direct result of our attitudes. That's right! Only 15 percent of success relates to our factual understanding and technical expertise. Attitude is the missing and most important success ingredient!

Why, then, do schools continue to spend 90 percent of their time and money developing the part of us that is responsible for just 15 percent of our success? If we are ever going to become successful and individually reach our ultimate capacity as human beings, we must readjust these percentages and start working on our attitudes. Your success starts when you do, and you start when you acquire a proper positive mental attitude.

"Born to Succeed"

A few days ago, my friend's wife had their first child — a beautiful, healthy, eight-pound baby boy, truly "born to succeed." After visiting the parents and child that evening in the hospital, I drove downtown to mail some letters at the post office before going home. On my way there, I witnessed a street scene that emphasized the importance of attitude.

As I approached the post office parking lot, I passed by four drunken bums leaning against the wall of a building. They were dirty and dressed in shabby clothing, and each was gripping a bottle of cheap wine as if it was his only friend. I had seen this type of thing before so their presence didn't affect me until I stopped at a traffic light and witnessed a contrasting scene.

As I sat there waiting for the signal to change, I noticed an opposite scene unfolding on the other side of the street. On the wall of a building was the sign, "Attorneys at Law." The doors to this building swung open, and in stunning contrast to the four bums, out came two successful-looking men dressed in three-piece suits walking on either side of a successful-looking, well-dressed woman. Then it hit me! The three experiences I'd had that night — seeing the baby in the hospital and then the bums and the attorneys — all fit together as the perfect example of the importance of attitude. Obviously mothers give birth only to boys or girls, and all babies are born to succeed. But never once has any mother given birth to an attorney, a businessman, a mechanic, a teacher, or a bum. Who and what we become is a direct result of who and what we think we can become. And by definition, these thoughts, this inner motivation and personal influence we have on ourselves, is called our attitude. Sure we're born to succeed, but we're not born with attitudes. We must acquire them. Attitude is the little thing that makes the big difference. Attitude is what determines our altitude. Attitude is what prepares you for the performance.

"Take Yourself Off the Shelf"

When I first started playing football at the University of Utah, I learned an important principle of life. We had played our first game on a Saturday and had been beaten by nearly twenty points by a much inferior team. It was now Monday and the team was assembled in the lecture hall to watch the game film. As the film showed play after play, the coach suddenly yelled, "Stop the projector! Run that play again!" The play was embarrasing and was definitely not a spectacular one to the players, but it impressed the coach so much that we ended up watching it seven times. The play consisted of the following: the opposing team had the ball; we were on defense. Their running back got the handoff and ran around the end, and our linebacker came up to tackle him. However, even though our guy hit the ball carrier with great force, the ball carrier continued to sprint down the field, never slowing a bit. Our guy just bounced off and missed the tackle! As the play continued to unfold, the ball carrier ran for twenty-five more yards until finally he was tackled and brought down from behind.

Now why was the coach so excited about this play? Because the same linebacker who missed the first tackle attempt (the guy who bounced off) was the guy who finally made the tackle twenty-five yards farther down the field! In other words, our man had given it his best effort once, had failed, but had gotten up and chased the halfback until he had finally stopped him.

After the seventh showing of the play, the coach turned on the lights and said, "This is my kind of guy! Coming into this game he was third string on the depth chart and wasn't even supposed to see any action. He only played because someone else got hurt. But now he will start for the rest of the season. I don't care what position he plays, but he will play! You see, this guy has the right attitude to be successful, and *when your attitude is right, your ability will always catch up!*" Then the coach concluded, "Take yourself off the shelf. All of you! Regardless of your present situation or ability, all of you need to take yourself off the shelf of mediocrity and complacency, and start working on your attitude."

Having the proper positive attitude is a must! But because of its importance and emphasis, sometimes it can be misused and abused. We should never try to fool ourselves or someone else by being unrealistic about positive thinking and attitude. It could get us into trouble.

There was a young man who wanted to become a champion boxer. In order for him to do so, he realized he must find a trainer to give him the necessary training. He did, and after several weeks of positive training, he finally scheduled his first fight. It was against an opponent who was much bigger than he was, but he didn't mind. He believed, "I can if I think I can." But instead of encouraging the boxer to work on his skills, the trainer emphasized only positive thinking.

Fight night came, and as the first round unfolded, our fighter was getting drilled — the big guy was really beating him up! When the round was finished, our guy staggered over to his corner, sat down on the stool, and asked his positive trainer how he was doing. The trainer replied, "You're doing great! Just keep thinking positive. The guy hasn't even hit you yet!"

The next round started and the same thing happened. The big man smashed and rearranged our guy's face in all shapes and sizes, hitting him with every blow. When the round finally ended, our fighter stumbled once again to his corner, sat down on the stool, and asked his trainer how he

23

was doing. The trainer again replied, "You're doing great! Just keep doing what you're doing. Think positive! The guy hasn't even hit you yet!"

To this the boxer replied, "Okay, but could you keep an eye on the referee, 'cause somebody out there's beatin' the tar out of me!"

Develop Positive Attitude and Skills

Positive attitude is essential in becoming successful, but it's of no worth unless we develop it to go hand in hand with our technical skills. At the same time, skills and knowledge do us no good unless we have the right attitude and motivation to use them. Both are necessary to achieving success.

What good does it do us if we know something and do nothing with that knowledge? For example, 6x7=42; that's essential to know, but if it only stays in our minds and no beneficial action follows, it's worthless! We don't learn merely to know — we learn to do! We learn so we can put our learnings into practice. Let's look at it another way.

When I was playing basketball in high school, I started a lot of games in the guard position. Therefore, I had to constantly handle the ball. On one particular occasion, I was bringing the ball up the court to begin our offense. Suddenly, the defensive man guarding me made an unexpected lunge at the ball. In response, I put a move on him like you wouldn't believe! It was awesome — the guy went cross-eyed! The only trouble was that I lost the ball.

The next time I got the ball, a similar thing happened. The guy tried to steal it, so I invented another dazzling move. However, as before, I lost the ball. During half time, our coach was obviously mad and taught me a great lesson. He said, "Clark, you've got all the moves, but you just can't get 'em out!" What he was saying was that it doesn't do any good to be able to invent the move if you can't execute it. It doesn't do you a bit of good if you make the move without the ball. To succeed, you have to have both the move and the ball — both the idea and the action that brings the desired result.

Unless you cultivate the knowledge, have the right attitude, and develop the tools, you will never be able to rise to any occasion, and you'll seldom achieve. In fact, opportunity may stare you in the face, but if no prior planning has preceded the performance, you will not recognize it and something like the following might happen to you.

Cecil Burns, the son of a Texas gambler, was born in a tent and grew up in and around the West. He never set any goals, had no material cravings of any sort, and had no ambitions other than hunting and fishing. He was content to be a drifter, and this lack of motivation gave him nothing more than an itinerant's life as a bum on Skid Row in Seattle, Washington. He was a committed client at the Salvation Army Harbor Light Mission.

Then one day an unbelievable thing happened to Cecil. A once-in-a-life opportunity not only stared him in the face, but actually grabbed him and filled his pockets.

At the age of fifty-six, Cecil hopped on a train to go wherever it would take him and ended up in Las Vegas, Nevada. On April 3, 1982, he walked into the Circus Circus Hotel and Casino and began playing a slot machine. A few minutes later he took a walk to stretch his legs. When he returned he found that someone else was using that machine.

While he was waiting for that machine, he plunked a few silver dollars into the nearby Silver Strike slot machine and hit the jackpot. Cecil Burns won $400,000 in cash and became instantly wealthy. In fact, this opportunity could have set him up financially for the rest of his life. All he had to do was put the money into a no-risk money market certificate at his local bank, offering (at that time) 15 percent interest, and he could have lived off the interest for the rest of his life. Before taxes, this income would have been $60,000 per year.

Now let me finish the story as it really happened. The night he won the money, Circus Circus gave him the royal suite. The next day he bought a new car and hired a chauffeur. Not only had he "made it," but he was going to "make it" even better. Leaving his car and driver behind, he caught a plane to Reno, Nevada, played the slots there, returned to Vegas, played there, and continued back and forth from Reno to Vegas for the next several days. During this week of weakness, Burns comments, "I lost and spent over $300,000 trying to hit another $400,000 jackpot, and I only hit little ones."

Sporting several days' growth of beard and being no different or better off than when he left, Cecil Burns returned to his friends and welfare handouts on Skid Row. What a waste! He returned in a new chauffeur-driven car with no money to buy more gas, and he returned to the same "no-future" life as if all of this had never happened.

Can you see now what I mean when I say we must acquire knowledge and develop tools to utilize the opportunities when they come? For if we're not prepared when opportunity comes, the ignorant Cecil Burns inside us will take over our chances for success and will mismanage our once-in-a-lifetime deal, too.

This motivating marriage between desire and know-how can be stressed in still another way. A musician, regardless of his desires and emotions, must possess an instrument and be able to play it in order to make his music come out. Likewise, an individual trying to make it in life also needs an "instrument" to let the music that's inside him come out. Herein lies the importance of this book. It not only will get you motivated, it will also give you the necessary "instruments" to implement your enthusiasm into action.

The net result: instead of being a motivated mass of indirection with your music stuck inside you, you will be a master of meaningful instruments which will allow all the music you can create to come out as beautiful rhyme and rhythm. You will no longer just be good; you'll be good for something.

This book is designed to help you accomplish this goal. It's a "do-it dictionary," a "behavioral bible," a "reality road map." It's a common-sense owner's manual for successful living. Therefore, to help you get the most out of it, you, the reader, need to agree with the following assumptions, or reading this book will do you no good.

Basics of This Book

1. Words are powerful. The average person will use half a billion words in his lifetime. Words rule mankind — they can change you and the world if you understand what they represent. For example: the short, three-letter word

spelled G-o-d does not stand out in any way. But when you consider what it represents and realize the enormous implications and symbolisms that come from it, it's enough to boggle the mind. Think about the impact words have had on the outcome of history — words like "Declaration of Independence," "Gettysburg Address," "Bill of Rights," or even simple one-liners such as "We Declare War," "I Love You," or "You Were Born to Succeed." When you understand that words are extremely powerful — that they move people and nations to do impossible things — you will let my words move you.

2. Believe in faith the words of this book. Understand that I'm not problem-conscious but solution-conscious. And know that the solutions written herein are tried and tested. Trust me and sincerely try what the book says. Don't merely read — do! Work it — it works! And concentrate!

In a Washington laboratory sits a great sun glass that measures three feet across. It's like a giant magnifying glass. This great glass gathers the rays of the sun that cover its flat surface and focuses them into a single point in space a few feet below. This single point of direct, concentrated sunlight is hotter than a blowtorch. It will melt and burn its way through a steel plate as easily as a red-hot paper clip burns through paper. In fact, this heat is so hot it cannot be measured, for it melts all instruments. And remember, it is just three feet of ordinary sunshine concentrated and focused on a single point. Scattered, these sun rays are hardly felt. But concentrated, they produce immeasurable power to melt through anything!

This principle also applies to human endeavor. Scattered, a man's energies seldom amount to much. Yet once they are focused on the task at hand, difficulties melt like ice cream on a hot stove. Form a habit of concentrating as you're reading this book. Focus all your energy on grasping, learning, and applying the principles found in it.

3. Life is given to each of us as a package deal. It's a trip through time that has a beginning and an end — a specific starting and stopping point. Each day is an extension of life, also with a beginning and an end, and it comes wrapped and delivered in exactly the same way. Because of this, each new day affords us the opportunity to celebrate a

new birthday — a "rebirthday" so to speak. It gives us a chance to be "reborn to succeed" — to have a fresh start and negotiate a new lease on living. In fact, every day — especially today because it's your "rebirthday" — makes clear the statement: "No matter what your past has been, you have a spotless future." Because today has a beginning and an end, take advantage of it. Use it to end your negative thoughts and negative actions; use it to end your lack of confidence and your fear of failure. Then use it to begin to replace your negativisms with positive affirmations. Use today to begin changing your "I can't" and "I won't" to "I will" and "I just did." Remember, "Today is the first day of the rest of your life." Why not make it a good, productive, positive day — the best it can possibly be!

4. Life is a story that can be told in story form. It's a story about people — people from all walks of life — tall people, short people, fat, skinny, and pretty people — rich, powerful, poor people — people of all races, colors, creeds, and affiliations. Therefore, any story told about someone else can also, one day, be told about you!

In order for you to understand this book, you must understand where I'm coming from.

5. Therefore, in conclusion, I want you to know of my genuine and sincere appreciation of you. I do care about you even though we may never have met. Thanks for caring enough about yourself, your community, and this great nation to seek out books like this one. For herein lies the potent words that will help you get started, "take yourself off the shelf," "train your brain," "tune up your tools," and motivate you to become the very best you can possibly be. Remember, you were "born to succeed." You were designed to "get high." And now I'm going to help you go for it!

Chapter Three

"You Were Born to Succeed!"

How to Become Successful

You were born to prevail, accomplish, gain, achieve, prosper, triumph, surmount, conquer, defeat, win. You were "born to succeed." And for you, this statement is true now more than ever before. America has been put in somewhat of a fix right now because of past misinformed "rebel" teenage generations who are now exercising their voting privileges without much knowledge of how our system works. However, in this country, anti-American, anti-establishment protests are over now and a conscientious effort is being made to curb this "free lunch" attitude. It's exciting to see the youth of America rise to this occasion. It's exciting to know that our generation is the generation that can turn this country around. And why can we? Because we understand that opportunity never knocks at anyone's door. *You* are opportunity — *you* open your own door!

Every one of us was born to succeed. Not born and forced to succeed, but born with the potential and opportunity to succeed. Whether or not success comes to us depends entirely on our desire and what we do with that desire. Success is a personal choice that anyone, anywhere, anytime can make. In fact, becoming successful and striving to be the best you can be is an essential goal for

every individual, even for the seemingly insignificant "little guy." Everyone is unique and extremely important, and everyone is part of the whole machine.

Who, Mx?

Xvxn though my typxwritxr is an old modxl,
It works quitx wxll, xxcxpt for onx of thx kxys.
Thxrx arx forty-onx kxyx that function, but
Just onx kxy not working makxs thx diffxrxncx.

Somxtimxs it sxxms that an organization is
Likx my typxwritxr — that not all of thx kxy
Pxoplx arx working propxrly.

You may say, "Wxll, I am only onx pxrson:
I don't makx or brxak an organization."
But a succxssful organization, to bx xffxctivx,
Rxquirxs thx activx participation of xvxry mxmbxr.

So thx nxxt timx you think that your xfforts arx not
Nxxdxd, rxmxmbxr my old typxwritxr and say to
Yoursxlf, "I am a vxry kxy pxrson in our organization,
And I am nxxdxd vxry much!"

This familiar typing exercise demonstrates *your* importance. It shows the importance of your learning to do your thing the best you can. It explains that regardless of your position in life, you have specific abilities — and a specific job to do. Countless others are depending on you to succeed because no one else has exactly what it takes to do what you're doing. When you fail to do your part, when you fail to do what only you can do, the organization cannot go on. In fact, life itself will not be full and rewarding (especially for others) because they missed out on what only you could offer. You see, it's true! Anyone and everyone was born to succeed and it's important to do so. Rich, poor, gifted, average, and even handicapped people all can and should be successful.

Ricky — Born to Succeed

A young boy living and growing up in Utah proved this. Ricky Newnan was a victim of cerebral palsy. At the time this story took place, he was fourteen years old, and because of his cerebral palsy, moved in motions that were very uncontrollable and uncoordinated. But did this stop him? No way!

31

Ricky's goal was to learn how to successfully ride his bicycle without training wheels. Early one morning he decided to make his dream of success come true, so he hopped on his bike and took off. Before he had gone very far he tipped over, flew over the handlebars, and skidded along the asphalt. Most of us would have just lain there. But Ricky didn't. He wanted to be successful! He hopped back on his bike, started to pedal it down the street, tipped over, flew over the bars, and again landed face first on the asphalt. It didn't matter, though. He wanted to succeed. Regardless of what it took, he was going to do it! So he hopped on his bike the third time, began to pedal, tipped over, and again landed on his stomach, face, and hands. Can you imagine the pain as he wiped the blood and gravel from his badly bruised body? Even after the eleventh and twelfth falls he refused to give up. He knew what he wanted and what he had to do to get it, and he was willing to go after it, no matter what. By nightfall, little Ricky Newnan had accomplished his goal and had made his dream come true. With most of his neighbors peeking out their windows through tear-filled eyes, Ricky made it all the way down the street without falling. He had definitely succeeded!.

In contrast, Harry Ruty tells of the fellow who was born with a silver spoon in his mouth but who never made much of a stir with it. This is typical of life, isn't it? All of us have the ability to succeed and most of us want to make it to the top. But very few ever do, especially those with extraordinary abilities, who certainly should. Why? It's because some never realize that success is a choice and, in fact, depends on the individual. Many feel that the world owes them something; that success should be given to them on a silver platter. And others who have already been successful once seem to feel they can forever ride on their past laurels. Hey, I know it sounds great, but it just isn't the way life is! Life is a constant climb toward success.

We Choose to Succeed

One of the greatest female athletes the world has ever known understood this and proved it to be true. Her name is Wilma Rudolph — an amazing black woman. I point out her skin color not because she's different, but to show that anyone from any background, from any race or color, can succeed!

Wilma Rudolph became famous when she made Olympic history as the first woman ever to win three gold medals in the same Olympic games. It was the 1960 Rome Olympics where Wilma proved herself to be the fastest woman in the world. She won the hundred-meter and two hundred-meter dashes in world record time, and then anchored the four-hundred-meter relay where the world's record was also shattered. One year after the games, Wilma continued to receive honors and dominate track meets as she broke the world's record in the sixty-yard dash, the seventy-yard dash, and the hundred-meter dash. In recognition of her amazing abilities, Wilma received a fitting tribute from the sports world that year. She was voted America's Female Athlete of the Year. This long list of gold medal performances and world record wins is fascinating, but it's not the wonder story I wish to tell. Wilma Rudolph's story begins many years earlier. You see, the true wonder is that she can even run at all.

When Wilma was born, she only weighed four and a half pounds and was expected to die. As she fought to survive, she was very susceptible to infections, and consequently, illness continually plagued her frail little body. At age four, the doctors discovered that her childhood sicknesses had left her crippled and unable to walk. A double attack of pneumonia and scarlet fever had left her with the use of only her right leg. It wasn't until she was eight years old that Wilma even barely began to walk, and this creeping walk was possible only if she wore a specially constructed, reinforced high-topped shoe. After receiving hundreds of long, lonely hours of therapy, which began when her mother drove her ninety miles to the doctor three days a week for over two years, Wilma was finally able to walk with a brace when she was twelve years old. By the time she was fifteen, she was the star of her high school basketball and track teams.

After three years of this kind of outstanding performance, she received a track scholarship to attend Tennessee State University, where she not only starred on

33

the track team, but also maintained a GPA of over 3.5. Beyond her college days, the rest of her story is in the record books. Talk about a winner — talk about determination and a proper positive mental attitude! Most people in her condition would have accepted the fact that they couldn't walk, that they were stuck, and they would have resorted to getting around in a wheelchair. But Wilma's attitude was different. She knew she was born to succeed and that she could someday walk. She believed positively that if she worked hard and was willing to pay the price, she could one day rehabilitate her leg to full strength and be like everyone else. She realized her potential and then went out and made her dreams come .true.

Wilma Rudolph truly discovered that it doesn't matter where you begin. All that matters is that you realize your inborn potential and commit to making the climb to the top.

I have always been excited about a story of one expedition to the top of Mount Everest. One of the details that seldom gets told is the reason why more people didn't make it to the top on this particular climb.

In this expedition, 150 men started the climb but only three made it to the top. Why? Who chose the lucky three who reached the summit?

As the climb proceeded for several days and upward over thousands of feet of elevation, weather conditions were constantly changing. Available oxygen became thin, and this caused nausea for many. As the days crept on, many questions about their abilities were thrown into the minds of the climbers — uncertainties like "I don't know if I can make it. Is it really worth all the agony and pain? I feel too sick to go on."

As these obstacles confronted the climbers, each had the choice of whether to give up and stop climbing, or hang in there and keep going.

So who chose the three men to go to the top? Who chose the three who were allowed to be successful, accomplish their goals, and make their dreams come true? No one did — they chose themselves!

You see, you do have a choice of whether or not to

succeed. It doesn't matter if you have tremendous potential to begin with or are presently below average, you can still become successful. All you have to do is take the time to sit down and think about your definition of what a successful person is. Decide what you want most for yourself and what you admire most in others. Implement what you think you should do and what you really want to do. And then remember that there are no shortcuts to success.

A prominent businessman who was enrolling his son in a major university shook his head in amazement when he began to read through the catalog listing course requirements. Trying to "pull some strings," he inquired of the counselor, "Does my son have to take all these classes? Isn't there something you can do to make it shorter? He wants to graduate quickly."

"Sure, he can take the shorter courses," answered the counselor. "But it all depends on what he wants to make of himself. When God makes a mighty oak tree, he takes twenty years. But he only takes two months to make a squash."

Success Through Constant Effort

Success takes time and requires "experience knowledge" from the school of real life. Napoleon Hill teaches this as he also uses an oak tree to define his law of success:

> If you wished a strong right arm, you could develop such an arm only by giving it the hardest sort of use.... The strongest oak tree of the forest is not the one that is protected from the storm and hidden from the sun. It's the one that stands in the open where it is compelled to struggle for its existence against the winds and rains and the scorching sun.

Success is not automatic, and it doesn't come overnight. There definitely is no shortcut. But it will come if you constantly give life your best effort and are willing to struggle through and endure all the bad weather. This is the key — constant effort and endurance to the end.

Success comes in life the way I perceive a football game. The game is not one big sixty-minute game, but a series of sixty to seventy little games or individual plays, played one at a time. Whether you are carrying the ball or playing defense, each play gives you the chance to succeed or fail.

At the last instant, you can choose whether to put every particle of effort into the running drive or tackle, or you can ease off. You can choose to succeed and hang in there every play or you can choose to fail, quit, and give up before the game is over.

Success is not a destination; it's a step-by-step process. Those who succeed are those who take things one step at a time. The Zen Buddhists believe, "The river does not flow." It is only several given moments in time put back-to-back in sequence. A verse whose author is unknown points this out from life:

> It took Michelangelo twelve years, one brush stroke at a time, to paint the scenes in the Sistine Chapel. It took Brahms twenty years, one note at a time, to compose his first symphony. It took Edmund Hillary eighty days, one step at a time, to climb the 29,000 feet of Mount Everest. Stroke by stroke, note by note, step by step, line upon line, precept upon precept — this is the secret to success.

Success also comes to those who "hang in there" one more time. We discussed taking one more step in Chapter 1, but this is different.

An exciting story about "hanging in there" is about a famous man who, when he first began a business, failed. The year was 1831. A year later he ran for a seat in the legislature and was defeated. The following year he failed in business again. Finally, in 1834, he was elected to the legislature but suffered a nervous breakdown two months later. During the next ten years he was defeated in elections for land officer, Speaker, and Congressman. In 1846, he was elected to Congress but was defeated for re-election in 1848. He failed in 1855 to gain a seat in the Senate and was defeated in 1856 when he ran for Vice-President. In 1858, he again failed to be elected a Senator. But finally, in 1860, he was elected President of the United States and became one of the greatest presidents this country has ever had! His name was Abraham Lincoln.

Some may say, "Lincoln's obstacles were only temporary and of the moment. No wonder he was able to hang in there and eventually become successful." But what about those who encounter a permanent obstacle or handicap? Are they still born to succeed and in the running for success?

Yes! If you are born to succeed, then you are born to succeed. There are very few exceptions!

My friend Richard Nelson knew he was born to succeed, and it was entirely because of this knowledge that he propelled himself on to overcome a devastating injury.

As a sixteen year-old junior at Manti High School in Manti, Utah, Richard was an outstanding athlete. He was the number two singles player on the state championship tennis team and had just made the basketball team that would go on that year to win the state championship. He was looking forward to much success as a senior the following season. But on October 23, 1966, most of his athletic future was suddenly taken away and his goals and dreams were put on the line.

Richard was riding his bicycle at night from Manti to Gunnison, Utah, to visit his girlfriend. The road was very steep in some places, which allowed Richard to pick up speed to about forty miles per hour. Because it was dark and difficult to see, Richard was following the white line on the shoulder of the road to ensure his safety. As he came around a blind curve and was looking down at the ground, Richard failed to see a car parked on his side of the road, jacked up to fix a flat tire. With no warning he hit the car and ended up in the hospital where he didn't regain consciousness until two days later. Besides bad cuts on his head and knee, his right collarbone and right arm were broken, and his arm was put in an L-shaped cast for two months. The cast came off on December 19 and Richard was given a series of tests to check the success of healing. He failed them. His triceps muscle had lost all of its strength — he could not push out with his arm. The doctor diagnosed that he had a pinched nerve and that the use of his arm might or might not come back. Richard's tiny right arm just hung at his side, and the doctors gave him no hope of recovery.

Because of his injury, Richard wasn't able to play on the basketball team that year, but the coach did make him equipment and statistics manager so he could still come to practice and be around the guys.

His junior year ended, the summer came, and Richard was determined to do what he had to do to make the basketball team the next year. He realized he couldn't make it right-handed, so he started working on his left-handed skills. All summer long, each and every night, he practiced on the baskets at the outdoor tennis courts in the center of town. Every night he shot 200 baskets left-handed and practiced dribbling and passing the ball. Instead of going to the school summer dances, Richard practiced basketball.

When the next season arrived, Richard was ready to try out for the team — and he made it! He never became a starter but was always the first substitute to go in the game.

The season boiled down to the final game of the year against Richfield High. This game would determine which team would win the league championship and advance into the state tournament playoffs. It was a "must" win for both teams.

Friday night came and the gym was packed. The starting guard for Manti had sprained his ankle earlier in the week, so Richard finally got his big break — he started the game! However, before the first quarter was over, Richard was replaced. It was hard to compete with the other players when he had to do it with only one arm. The game continued on until the last minute, when Richard was finally sent back in. It turned out to be perfect timing! With forty seconds left to play, Richard got the ball and a Richfield player fouled him. He stepped up to the free-throw line in a "one and one" situation (if he made the first foul shot, he would get a chance to shoot and make a second basket). Confidently, Richard picked up the ball, braced it in his left hand, and shot. Swish! He made it and the crowd went wild! He then made the next shot, bringing Manti High to within one point of Richfield. The crowd stood and went crazy again!

Richfield then took the ball out of bounds and threw a long pass down court to try and score a quick, easy basket. But with his undying determination, Richard leaped in the air to intercept the pass. When he landed he was fouled again, giving him another "one and one" opportunity at the free-throw line. With fifteen seconds left on the clock, Richard balanced the ball in his left hand, took a deep

breath, and shot. The crowd was deathly quiet until —
swish! He tied the game! His next shot went up — and down
— and through! Swish again! He made it — left-handed!
Richard Nelson won the game and became the hero of the
school! And how and why was he able to do it? Because he
firmly believed he was born to succeed and was willing to
hang in there one more time until his belief became reality.

These stories are great, but what if you got into trouble
when you were young, got off on the wrong foot, and knew
there was no way to change and succeed? Is there still hope
for you to fulfill your "born to succeed" birthright?

From Slums to Judge

Joseph Serrentino, a juvenile court judge from Los
Angeles, California, proves *yes* with his own incredible
story.

His home was in Brooklyn. He was the second eldest in a
family of seven children, and grew up in an atmosphere of
street gangs and Mafia killers. By the time he was twenty
years old, Joe had served time in reform school, in jail, in
the brig, and even in a padded cell for incorrigibles. He
flunked out of school four times, went through nearly
thirty jobs, and was literally kicked out of the Marines.

As a dropout with no skills and in need of money, he tried
his hand at professional boxing. He soon quit this as well.

One day, as he was passing Brooklyn's Erasmus Hall
High School, Joe saw a sign that invited passersby to enroll
in night school. Suddenly he realized that his only chance
for a better life was through education, and his
inadequacies hit him like a ton of bricks.

So Joe signed up, found he loved to learn, and graduated
with the highest grade-point average in the history of the
night school. He then decided to attend the University of
California at Santa Barbara, where he became student
body president and graduated magna cum laude. After
graduation, he began reviewing his life with all its defeats
and decided there was one more thing he should do before
he tackled the real world. He re-enlisted in the Marines to
remove that bad, embarrassing blemish from his record.
After an honorable discharge, he entered Harvard Law
School and graduated as valedictorian of his class in 1967.

His valedictory address touched everyone present as he recounted his life story and concluded with these words: "Do not look mainly for tragedy or trauma to explain this change; it was mainly resolution from within. I decided I wanted to change and be successful, and I did."

Privileged Americans

From these stories we learn that in these dynamic individuals is perpetuated that same unconquerable spirit de Tocqueville once discovered in the American character: "In his eyes what is not yet done is only what he has not yet attempted to do." And in the 150 years since this was written, the climate has never been better for doing the undone. If anyone has ever been born to succeed or ever been given a fair chance to succeed, today's generation of young Americans has.

We, as Americans, are a blessed people. We have more going for us than all the other countries in the world combined. We have the highest standard of living, and more successful people per capita, than any nation on earth. In fact, the average American newspaper boy working part time earns more money than 50 percent of the people in the entire world! Don't misunderstand me — I'm not saying success is measured only in money. But it definitely is one reward people pursue. In fact, becoming a millionaire is one of the grandest of the fabled American dreams and seems to be an accepted way for us to prove we were born to succeed.

An Optimistic Side to the Depression

Because of this, and because so much negativism is emerging from our society about a recession, a depression, and a "no-hope" pessimistic projection for our economic future, I wish to point out something. Even though these may appear to be bad economic times, these may actually be the best of times for making a million dollars. A recent Merit report found that over 50 percent of those surveyed believed they were born to succeed and felt that it was still possible for an individual to start out poor in America and become wealthy through sacrifice and hard work. And this belief has been put into practice as the number of millionaires in America has tripled in the last ten years!

The latest statistics furnished by the U.S. Trust Company in New York show there are over 630,000 millionaires in the country today. Compare this to a government estimate totalling 180,000 in 1972, and you have an average annual growing rate of over 14 percent since then.

I know many of you are saying, "Sure there are millionaires — lots of them — but they inherited their wealth; they got their money from Daddy." This is no longer the rule. According to the U.S. Trust Company, most of today's millionaires originally possessed only new ideas and a desire to work.

For example, in 1977, two quasi-hippies, barely twenty-one years old, spotted a need for mini home computers and decided to fill it. Stephen Wozniak and Steven Jobs managed to dig up $1,300 between them to develop their first machine, and out of their California garage came Apple Computer. Sales were more than $2 million in 1977 and soared to $583 million by 1982. In just six years, a two-man operation has grown into a multinational corporation with 3,391 employees. Steven Jobs, Apple's very young president, has become worth $150 million.

Mo Seigel started Celestial Seasonings in Boulder, Colorado. His product? Herbal tea. His annual sales reached $13 million before he was twenty-five years old.

Women are doing it, too! In 1977, at the age of twenty-one, Debbie Fields started Mrs. Fields Cookies. In 1982, her company, with seventy stores from Chicago to Hawaii, sold 90 million chocolate chip cookies, with sales reaching 30 million dollars. And Debbie Fields is only twenty-six years old!

You see, everyone was born to succeed, and those who do are those who decide to work hard until success comes — in work, in school, in athletics, in life. The formula for success is always the same.

As we've already mentioned, you were born to succeed, but you're not compelled to end up that way. Success is an action course, not a passive one. Success comes not only by will power, but also by understanding — by being able to see the methods and believe in the techniques that work. For example, success is found in life as a young boy finds it in learning to ride a bicycle. As long as he is moving forward, he maintains his balance. When he stops, the bike tips over.

Fighting for Success, Not Defending It

In addition, once we are successful, we can't slow down and glide on our past laurels. Success is found and maintained as we continue to strive for excellence. This explains the "underdog psychology" in sports. When the members of a championship team start to think of themselves as *the* champions" or *the* competition," they lose their competitive edge. They no longer have something to fight for but instead they have a ranking or position to defend. The champions' role is suddenly reversed from fighter to defender as they feel they've arrived and have nowhere else to climb to. The underdog often brings about an upset of this championship team because the underdog is still fighting for something.

If you work hard and become successful, and if you do become a champion, don't be content to defend it. Remember that every time you compete, you're not defending your champion status — you're fighting for it! You no longer have it once the competition starts; you've put it on the line (up for grabs) and must fight to get it back again.

Is there a specific conclusion that can be drawn from the many examples we've listed in this chapter? Yes!

Success is not limited to social status, economic class, ancestral origin, sex, race, color, creed, neighborhood, or family inheritance. Rather, it is within the grasp of every person — rich or poor, famous or common, male or female, old or young, crippled or healthy, who is willing to take a risk, work hard, and hang in there because they know they were *born to succeed!*

Chapter Four

"What Is Your Problem?"

How to Overcome Peer Pressure and Fear,
Deal with Cliques, Attract Friends,
Be Popular with the Opposite Sex, and
Better Communicate with Your Parents

Have you ever done something a little weird or perhaps even "blown it" so bad that people swear you are a bit "off the wall"? You know the feeling when people look at you as though you were a bit "wiggy"; as though you didn't have both paddles in the water.

When someone does witness your miserable foul-up, oftentimes they react by pulling a disgusted face while sneering as they ask you, "What is your problem?" Sound familiar? If so, you're normal. It happens to all of us. But usually when it happens it offends us and give us more of a complex. That's right, I said *more* of a complex. Everybody, regardless of how beautiful, rich, powerful, or famous they are, has something they don't like about themselves, and this sudden awareness is spreading a rapidly-growing inferiority complex epidemic throughout society. Our complexes are adversely affecting our lives as we continuously compare ourselves with others. Believe me, I know about complexes! When I was in high school I

WHAT IS YOUR PROBLEM ?
Peer Pressure
Find out who you are
What you represent
How Can I Be Popular
Deal with CLIQUES
Make others feel Important
Good
Wanted
Listen
Don't be phony
Be honest - self & others
Be Consistently YOU
Don't Be Your Own Problem
Discover Solutions
Fear
Face it head on
If you want a quality-Act like you have it

had so many pimples they sent me home for fear I had chicken pox, and when I finally came back, I still had so many that when I fell asleep in my math class, the kids played connect-the-dots on my face! Complexes affect everyone, because everyone has problems.

Don't Get Discouraged

Therefore, you shouldn't let "What is your problem?" get you discouraged. Instead you should look at this abrupt inquiry as a very positive, stimulating experience and use it to your best advantage. For in this single question lies a series of solutions to life's ups and downs. Let me show you what I mean.

First solution. You need to recognize that you are your own problem just as I am my own problem. Therefore, accept yourself for who you are, realize that you're unique and special, and get excited about what you can eventually become. Be yourself. You can only offer what you have.

Second solution. As you work for your goals, remember that there is opposition in all things. Therefore, you win some and you lose some. Your problem might be failing or losing more than most. If it is, realize that the law of averages guarantees that if you continue to seek success, eventually you will win your share of the time. Don't use excuses like "I'm poor or uneducated or disabled" to explain your failures. If you're failing, just continue to work harder until you "fail" your way to success.

Thomas Edison started as a newsboy on trains and "failed" his way to success by becoming the greatest inventor in history. He was the greatest because he conducted more experiments that failed than anyone else, and therefore he was successful his share of the time.

Henry Ford built an auto empire by starting out making $2.50 a week. Sir Isaac Newton discovered many important things, including the law of gravity. But he was a poor farm boy whose father died before he was born and whose mother had to raise him on an income equivalent to about $400 a year. He had plenty of excuses but used none of them. Some of our greatest and most famous athletes started out as crippled, handicapped, or below

45

average weaklings and became world champions. So don't lean on excuses; instead, balance on effort!

Third solution. Understand that people need to feel important. One of the biggest problems we have is always trying to act more important than we really are. Think about how true this is. There are a lot of people driving around with trailer hitches on their cars, and they don't even own anything to pull!

Fourth solution. Don't be locked in, tied down, or so habit-bound that you can't see any possibilities for betterment. Don't think there is only one way of doing something. When you're like this you're known as "regular as a goose goes barefoot." And the longer you stay stubborn, refuse to accept change, and stop seeking new ways to grow, the longer you'll stay average and fail in life. Remember, the person who has stopped growing has just plain stopped.

At an exhibit in a county fair was a pumpkin grown in the exact shape of a gallon jug. The farmer explained, "When this pumpkin was no bigger than my finger, I put it into the jug and let it grow. When it filled the jug, it stopped growing." Our closed minds do to us what the walls of the jug did to the pumpkin.

If you keep these four solutions in mind as you now ponder the following questions and answers, you'll be able to change your present thinking, opportunities, situations, and future. You'll have the answers to every "What is your problem?" question.

The following are four of the most popular questions asked by young people today.

Peer Pressure

How can I overcome peer pressure? How can I learn to say no?

Realize there are two ways to be controlled and influenced: from within and from without; by you and by others. The solution to peer pressure, then, is finding out who you really are and what you really represent. Only then will you know what you want to be. As you learn this, others won't be able to adversely affect your actions. In fact, you probably won't even associate with others who don't act or think like you do and, therefore, you'll avoid outside pressure altogether.

But remember, if the things you think about are different from the things you do, you'll never be happy. When you're consistently yourself in thought, word, and action, peer pressure will never affect you, and the next time someone wants you to participate in something "uncool," you will be able to say no.

Fear

How can I overcome fear?

Fear is real. Fear of failing, fear of what others may think, fear of a new school, fear of dating and dancing, fear of taking tests, fear of police officers, fear of dentists and doctors. The list goes on and on. Fear is real and it's not something that just goes away. We can't merely ignore fear or try to avoid it. If we are ever going to overcome fear, we must face it head on.

What is fear? Zig Ziglar defines fear to be false evidence appearing real. In other words, fear is worrying about the consequences of something bad happening when in reality it usually doesn't happen. The assumptions only appear real. Fear or worry has been broken down as follows: 40 percent of our worries never happen, 30 percent are in the past and cannot be changed, 12 percent are needless health worries, 10 percent are miscellaneous (about anything and everything), and only 8 percent are actually real.

The easiest solutions I know of to the problem of overcoming fear are found in the words of Ralph Waldo Emerson and William James. Emerson: "If you do the thing you will have the power." William James: "Act as if — and you will feel or be that way." Joined together, the advice would be to act as if you're not afraid by going ahead and doing whatever you fear. And as you do, you must realize that obviously there will be some rejection and failure to adequately perform, and this will hurt. However, the more times you attempt the task or experience the situation you fear, the deeper the callous grows over the wound and the more you become immune to rejection. Soon you will be so accustomed to failing that little will bother you. Besides, by now you will be a "seasoned veteran," an expert in what you're doing, and therefore, you'll seldom fail.

Generally, most people find the everyday fears we've discussed a bit uncomfortable but bearable, and they won't go to extremes to avoid having to deal with them.

Phobias

However, what about those who have a phobia, a specific and very high degree of fear which is out of proportion and unrealistic? He or she will almost always go to great personal inconvenience to stay away from whatever causes the phobia reaction. The following is part of a long list of phobias that someone (including yourself) might encounter:

Claustrophobia — the fear of close quarters.

Ochlophobia — the fear of crowds.

Ailurophobia — the fear of cats.

Anthropophobia — the fear of people.

Cynophobia — the fear of dogs.

Now let's try to understand what they are, how they occur, and how to overcome them.

The phobia is a unique defense system created in the mind. When the victim recognizes a situation as threatening, the phobia reaction tells the person to avoid it. And because he avoids whatever makes him uncomfortable, he perpetuates his phobia on and on.

The phobia condition occurs when a specific threatening act or event, usually an early-life experience dealing with disapproval, fright, or rejection, happens that devastates the child to the degree that he never forgets it. And the lifelong effects of such events prove that he doesn't.

Because these extreme fears enormously affect the life of the victim, he must understand how to deal with them and overcome them. Until recently, phobias were treated only with psychotherapy to identify the original cause of the phobia. This is a good start, but definitely is not adequate. Doctors can help, but you are the only one who has the inner ability to overcome the phobia.

After you pinpoint the origin and if you truly want to overcome the fear, the only resources you need are the ability to relax and the willingness to use your imagination. For example, you have claustrophobia. To overcome it, you need to go to a calm, quiet place and sit in a comfortable, relaxed position. Then imagine yourself in a very small, stuffy, dark, boxed-in room. At first, you may be able to stay relaxed for only a short time before the imagined phobic situation gets to you. But as you continue to practice this exercise called "desensitization therapy," you not only will overcome the fear in your imagery, but also you will eventually rid yourself of it in real life.

If you have a fear of dogs, don't start imagining German shepherd police dogs. Start your desensitization with a puppy. If your fear is cats, don't start with a lion. Imagine a cute kitten and go from there. This therapy works with all phobic conditions if taken seriously and performed systematically. It has worked in my life and it can in yours too.

Being Popular, Dealing with Cliques

How can I be popular?

Being popular seems to be a most important part of growing up. I think a person is popular because of certain qualities. Regardless of whether you are blonde or brunette, short or tall, or skinny or fat, you can become or remain popular if you actively cultivate and develop the following characteristics:

1. Bring out the best in others when they're around you. Allow them to be just themselves. Let them feel that being with you is positive and worthwhile. Make them honestly say, "I like me best when I'm with you."

2. Always make people feel they are sincerely wanted and important, that they have something special and unique to offer.

3. Do more empathetic listening than talking. People love listeners.

4. Don't be phony; anyone can see right through it. Be genuine and sincere.

5. Don't trifle or play with the hearts of the opposite sex; don't ever lead anyone on and play "mind games."

6. Be honest in all your dealings with your fellowmen and women.

7. Be honest with yourself. Be able to laugh at yourself.

49

8. Don't backbite or gossip. Look for only the good in others.

9. Be consistently you — not wild around wild people and straight around straight people. Always be the same; people respect you for that.

If you want to be popular, remember that you can't please everyone and you can't expect everyone to like you. Therefore, first discover and define yourself before you select the type of individuals you want to be with and who share your goals, ideals, and habits. If you're doing the things that interest you and others are doing the same, eventually your paths will cross and you'll become popular with one another.

All in all, the single most important thing to remember as you search for popularity is never to compromise your beliefs, and especially your morals, just because you think it will make you popular. You might feel popular for the time being, but others will soon realize that you're weak, and they won't want to associate with you anymore. Then, instead of being popular, you will be laughed at, people won't respect you, and you will have made yourself sick.

How can I deal with cliques?

Dealing with cliques is another very important matter because they are everywhere. You can find them in athletic teams, dance clubs, "druggie" groups, orchestras and bands, social parties, and honor societies. There is a specific clique for every type, group, and individual you can think of.

Cliques seem to be important to us, but when you really analyze them, they are no big deal. They are nothing more than groups of people who are somewhat insecure in their thinking and actions and who need to constantly be around their peers in order to feel important, strong, accomplished, and together. I was in some cliques, and I wanted to be in others where I was not invited. I was just like you are now. For this reason, let me share how I handled cliques. It really works!

If you know who you are, where you are going, and how you're going to get there, you definitely don't need the kind of support that you get from membership in a clique. As you become successful in what interests you — sports, music, dance, motorcycles, cars, math, English, science, astronomy, etc. — you'll be, in effect, forming your own "clique" as others start wanting to associate with you.

If you want to become a part of a certain clique, evaluate the members' behavior to see if it meets your own standards and interests. Then, if it does, become the best you can be at what you and they can do. The natural consequence will be full acceptance by the whole crew. Not just because you are a member of the clique, but because you're good at what they like to do. Remember, everyone likes to be around successful, winning people.

One of the most popular boys in my school was a big, heavy "roly-poly" guy who couldn't do anything particularly well. But he did have the quality to laugh at himself. Because of this, my friends and I got to know him well. We discovered what a great human being he was and how much better we could become by being friends with him. Therefore, he became everyone's friend and a member of everyone's clique — not because of looks or talents, but because of personality.

This brings us to the question, "How can I attract friends?" Being able to laugh at yourself is one sure way of attracting people to you. Everyone seeks out and enjoys a funny, good-natured friend. But I found out some other attractive traits that are also effective and important. My survey indicated that most guys and girls try to talk wild and act big around their friends, but when I got them by themselves, these traits were most important to them:

What Boys Like About Girls — What Is Attractive to Them

1. A girl who has enough self-respect to take care of herself. You can tell a lot about people by the way they dress, comb their hair, polish their shoes, wash their hands, brush their teeth, and use deodorant and perfume. All guys are attracted to well-groom, good-smelling women, but take it easy on the make-up. Girls should look natural, not too painted. Girl (referring to her jacket): "How do you like my new coat?" Boy (looking at her face): "Fine, only you've got it on too thick."

51

Clothes don't have to be expensive, but they must be clean. You don't have to be skinny, but you must not be fat. If you are a big girl with big bones, that's fine. However, unless it's a medical problem, there is absolutely no reason to be overweight. If you want to be attractive, then exercise, watch your calories, and stay in shape. It doesn't matter how much you weigh; what matters is how you look.

2. A girl who wants to be the best she can be. She is motivated and goal-oriented. She doesn't concentrate on getting dates and impressing boys. She's not only involved with school and good grades, but also she works on other interests such as handwriting, typing skills, music, painting, sewing, dance, skiing, tennis, swimming, jogging, racquetball, gymnastics, or whatever. She reads to expand her mind and keep current. She inspires others to be better as she constantly betters herself. She is challenging to be around and she motivates others to accomplish more.

3. A girl with an outgoing personality. Girls don't need to be introverted; they can act any way they choose to. A girl should be able to laugh at herself, spread an infectious smile, and be courteous, gracious, and sincere. She should be willing to make the first move of a relationship, such as starting things rolling with a "Hello" or a "Maybe we could study sometime." Guys are shy just like girls are. If a girl doesn't say something or make a move, how is a boy supposed to know she's interested? Don't be loud and giddy and don't talk too much about yourself. Guys are attracted to girls who are confident and who make them feel strong, important, and needed. Selectively feed the male ego and you'll have him "whipped" forever.

4. A girl who doesn't have to be impressed by boys. A girl who allows him to be just himself, who accepts him for who and what he is. She doesn't compare him with other guys and she gives him her undivided attention when she's out on a date with him.

5. A girl who uses her brain and doesn't rely on only her looks or her fancy car to get her through life. This grows old too fast. Guys like "mystery" women. A girl doesn't need to flaunt herself in order to appear sexy and attract boys. Girls who also want to be intriguing sometimes wear

longer dresses, their hair up, boots, and perhaps even glasses. These women are much more attractive and desirable to be with than those who expose everything, including a poor self-image.

What Girls Like About Boys — What Is Attractive to Them

1. A guy who is strong, not necessarily physically, but mentally and emotionally. He must be able to hold up under pressure and perform a duty with discipline, hard work, and stability. Girls don't like to be around "Herbert Milktoasts," and they constantly notice guys that are. When they go out with you, they want to feel secure. Girls and their parents are attracted to guys who are responsible enough to work hard in school. This tells them the guy will also be responsible with himself and with their daughter.

2. A guy who is athletic-looking. He doesn't have to be an athlete to look like one. Anyone can exercise and get his body in good shape. Girls like firm shoulders, arms, and waists; this makes them feel more feminine and secure. There is nothing worse than an overweight-here, too-skinny-there guy who gets kissed at the door only because he is so out of breath from climbing up the front steps that he needs mouth-to-mouth resuscitation to make it back to his car.

3. A guy who treats his mother like a queen. Most of the time, after a long relationship, guys treat their girls like they treat their mothers. Girls are aware of this. Therefore, they don't want to associate with guys who are rude to their moms and other women. Girls like to be pampered and cared for. They like their doors opened, their coats helped on, their chairs pulled out at meals. Girls like polite, kind, considerate guys. If you really want to be "macho," be sensitive and lovable. Say "thank you" and "please," don't be afraid to show emotion, and never take anything for granted.

4. A guy who is a "creative dater." Girls are turned off by the regular "movie and pizza" routine, and are especially turned off if the guy feels the girl owes him something

more than a simple "thank you." You can have a great time without going to the "submarine races." Girls want to be with you, but they want to have a variety of activities. For example: go bowling, get Chinese food. Go canoeing, get Mexican food. Go hiking, take peanut butter and honey sandwiches. Go to a play or a concert, have an elegant dinner, and go straight home. Get a group of friends together and have a party, a study class, or a dance. Go bike riding, visit a museum, take a ride on a train. Organize a progressive dinner — go from house to house, eating a different course of the meal at each location. Double date, triple date. Go out with your parents and families to family dinners, outings, and reunions. It's *cool* to be seen with family. You see, there is a lot to do!

5. A guy who doesn't compare his date with other girls. Guys should always make the girl they're with feel like a queen, like she is the most important thing to him on that particular date. Guys shouldn't flirt with other girls while they're with their date. Girls are turned off by guys who gossip and backbite. This makes them wonder what the guy says about them when they're not around. Girls are attracted to guys who let them be themselves, who don't expect the girl to change just to suit them.

6. A guy who doesn't "throw the lines" on girls and try to flatter them or "put the moves" on them as is mentioned in Number 4 above. Girls know what's going on and can see right through "lines" and insincere actions. Example — Boy (as he and his date drive along a lonely road): "You look lovelier to me every minute. Do you know what that means?" Girl: "Yeah, I bet you're about ready to run out of gas."

Child-Parent Communication

How can I better communicate with my parents?

This final question seems to be a growing major concern. Communicating is an exact science. By this I don't want to turn you off by its simplicity, but I do want to stress the important and intricate ways to communicate effectively. To be successful, you need to increase your awareness of how you relate to and communicate with significant people in your life. Having relationships and friendships not only with peers but also with parents is crucial to our growth as individuals.

What is a relationship? To me, two people have a relationship when they have a history together and anticipate some kind of future. This is definitely true in the case of parent-child relations. Knowing that everything we do or say is building up or tearing down our relationship for the future will make us constantly look for and work on better ways to improve and enrich the relationship. This is where the art of communication comes in. All relationships are successful or unsuccessful depending on how well we communicate. There is no such thing as a generation gap; it's only a communication gap.

Communicating with parents is easy and very exciting. All you have to do is remember five points.

1. Be extremely empathetic. Before you even begin your conversation, imagine yourself as parents and think back on their experiences. Truly try to understand where they're coming from.

2. Participate in the home and family setting. Help with the work — washing dishes, cleaning the house, doing yard work, etc. This relieves tensions and jealous feelings among brothers and sisters and loosens up Dad when you need to borrow the car or want some help with your homework. When you are willing to help and get along with others, they are just as willing to help you and make things run smoothly. When you help, there's always time to talk to Dad and Mom.

3. Now that you've established common ground on which to communicate, you need to develop and always maintain a truthful, totally trusting relationship. No matter what happens, and regardless of how hard it is to confess or talk about it, never tell a lie — especially to your parents. Always tell the truth and be open with your feelings and thoughts. Don't be afraid to show emotions and especially don't hold back saying "I love you." These three words do more for opening up the lines of communication than any others. "I'm sorry" and "please forgive me" work wonders as well.

4. Always make your parents feel important. Be proud of them in public — introduce them to your friends. Get them

involved in your world, in your activities, and in your successes and failures. By letting them know what's happening in your life, they can better counsel you when you need help and direction. If they understand where you are coming from (clothes styles, other parents' dating rules, peer pressure problems, etc.), you can open up the lines of communication and help them understand your challenges.

5. The last point to remember in developing good communication skills is to learn to listen. That means listen — don't just hear. Listen to your parents' advice. Listen to their stories and their experiences. Listen to why they say what they do and why they want you to do something. I guarantee your parents don't want you to fail any more than you do.

Now that you have answers and solutions to "What is your problem?" you need not ever make another excuse. Just change your actions by using these answers in your everyday life. Remember, the only problem you have is *you*. Only you can decide how you will be. And because you were born to succeed, all you have to do now is do it!

Chapter Five

"Am I Winning or Losing?"

How to Always Win

In 1971, a young boy in Worthing, Texas, went to see the doctor. After examining him, the doctor said that he was anemic and he would never be able to participate in interscholastic sports competition. He was lucky just to be alive.

But the boy had a dream to play football, so he had to figure out a way to prove the doctors wrong. As a freshman he told his father about his dream. At the time his dad was a minister in a religion that didn't believe in or allow contact sports, but because of his desire to help his son, he quit the ministry and became a truck driver.

In his freshman year the boy was disappointed when the coaches told him he was too small and weak to play. So he became the team manager. But after every practice the boy stayed late to run laps and windsprints, trying to get his frail body into better physical condition. At the end of his freshman year he went to his dad and told him, "I have one goal. I want a uniform like the rest of the guys." During his sophomore year he got the uniform but never played in a game.

In his junior year he again went to his dad with another goal: "I want to get into one game." The last game of the season, Worthing High was thirty points ahead and he got to play the whole fourth quarter.

Are You Winning or Losing ?

This one is Completely full

This one has the same Volume of Water

Which One has Reached its full Capacity?

We Cannot Compare Ourselves With Others −!

if we do −−

We Fail To Fill up Our Talent Tumblers!

At the beginning of his senior year he told his dad about another goal. He wanted to play in every game and earn a scholarship to a major college. At season's end, he was recruited by two schools — Baylor University and Texas Tech. Texas signed their first two prospects but Baylor didn't, so they took him on a risky long shot.

During this boy's first year, Baylor lost three linebackers by the fourth game and he was moved up as the starting middle-linebacker. In his sophomore year he was All-Southwest Conference and in his junior and senior years he was a unanimous choice for All-American. He was selected by the Chicago Bears in the second round of the National Football League college player draft and is now the starting middle-linebacker. His name is Mike Singletary. A kid who was barely alive and wasn't supposed to play competitive sports became one of the best linebackers in the country.

We Are What We Think We Are

This example illustrates a very crucial point about life. We are what we think we are. I didn't say that we are what we do. This is false and dangerous to assume and is a very different statement. If we are what we do, what happens if we become injured or crippled or are laid off from our job? To understand the difference between these two statements, we need to separate *being* from *doing*. More than anything, we are what we feel — we are who and what we think we are.

This is why Mike Singletary gradually progressed and changed into the best linebacker around. In spite of what others thought of his potential, he saw himself as a top-notch football player and acted accordingly. He became exactly what he thought he was.

I make this point because the essence of winning and losing is determined by how we see ourselves. In order for us to win or become champions, we must first see ourselves as winners and champions.

What are champions? Let's define them.

Champions aren't great all the time, but they are great when they need to be. Champions understand their capacities and their abilities. They overcome the odds and

59

rise to the occasion when they have to. That's why champions seldom buckle under pressure. In fact, to a champion, pressure doesn't exist. Pressure is not something that is naturally there. It's created when you question your own ability. And when you know what you can do, there's never any question.

Champions aren't born, they are made through hard work and determination. They are made of fighting hearts and burning desires. They are made when an individual discovers his own ability and decides to do what he can do in the best way he knows how. In other words, champions give it everything they've got when less would be sufficient.

Because champions are made, it doesn't matter what your interests or talents are. Each of you can become a champion. There are champions all around us — in sports, music, school, business, service to others.

All of us were born with the ability to succeed. All of us can make it to the top because we have the tools to become champions. But whether we do or not is our choice. We can choose to use those tools to reach our ultimate capacities as human beings, or we can let them rust and never make our dreams come true. What are you going to do? You can become a champion if you want to. Remember, you were "born to succeed"!

Each day on TV and radio, sportscasters tell us about championship performances involving champion individuals who know they were born to succeed. Now I know some of you may not be interested in sports. But if you think about it, you and I go through life the same way these champion athletes go through a great race or a great game. What makes a champion is always the same, regardless of the field of interest. This is what this chapter is about.

We're all neighbors now — every living human. You and your friends are as much a part of the world as I am, and we have a responsibility to make sure it is a decent place to live. But in order to make the world the best it can be, each of us needs to do our part; each of us needs to become the best we can possibly be.

It won't be long before our generation will be running this planet. *We* will be making the decisions and choosing our leaders. Therefore, our generation has to do a better job than our parents, just as their generation did a better job than the generation before it. That's what being a champion is all about — learning from the past, giving it your best shot, never giving up, and truly becoming the very best you can be.

What you do with your life means a great deal to me and to everyone else, and it should mean much to you. You see, we're all in this life together. It's a team effort! Even though we may have come to America on different ships originally, we're all in the same boat now. The world is counting on us and we must succeed.

Now I realize that everyone understands this and that if we surveyed one thousand people, we would find that everybody wants to win, everybody wants to be a champion, and everybody wants to pay the price to get there. But few people really ever do. Why? What separates the winners from the losers? The answer is simple: winners know that *wanting* to pay the price is a start but it's not enough. They understand that you also have to be *willing* to pay the price. Wanting to win is the dreaming part — the thinking part. But it's of no value unless you're also willing to prepare — willing to enjoy the price of success. If you're truly willing to pay the price, then you'll realize the price is no inconvenience at all. Champions understand the benefits and know the sweat, toil, and momentary pain they suffer now is a bargain for what is to come.

Eric Heiden, one of the American Olympic champions in the 1980 Winter Games, won five gold medals as a speed skater. Because Wisconsin winters are so brutal, Heiden had a practice platform constructed indoors. Four hours a day, six days a week, he skated back and forth, back and forth, training month after month, to develop his long, smooth, winning stride.

ABC sports television went to Wisconsin to film his training sessions. When they focused on his strength, rhythm, and determination, it gave you "goose bumps." And then the camera showed his face. One might expect his expression to be strained or complaining, but not Eric Heiden. He was a winner! There was no anguish or sacrifice. On Heiden's face was a big smile.

Staged for the camera?

No — what you didn't see behind the cameraman, in complete view of Eric Heiden, was a big picture of five Olympic gold medals.

Eric didn't pay any price; he gave willingly because he knew the benefits were worth more than the effort. He willingly paid the price now so he could enjoy the price forever.

If you choose to be a winner as Eric did, you should strive to be a winner every day. You should form a habit of spending the hours of each day in the best way you know how, the way a winner would.

> God has given me this day
> To use as I will.
> I can waste it or use it for good.
> What I do this day is very important
> Because I'm exchanging it for a day of my life.
> When tomorrow comes
> This day will be gone forever, leaving
> Something in its place I have
> Traded it for. I want it
> To be gain, not loss, good not evil,
> Success not failure, in order that
> It shall be worth the price
> I paid for it.

Author Unknown

Did I Win or Did I Lose?

If you think about your life and what you want to do with it, I'm sure you'll agree with me that at the end of each day, all of us need to know the answer to the question, "Did I win or did I lose?" It's the way we keep score and plot our progress.

This fact intrigues me. What is winning and what is losing? Why are some people winners and others losers? Do losers have a chance to win?

Defined, a loser is one who suffers deprivation, who fails to use; who wastes; who wanders from and does not maintain; and who fails to win. A winner is defined simply as one who wins; a victor; a champion. Let's relate these definitions to our personal situations.

For much of my life I didn't know what it meant to be a winner or loser. And, to be honest, it really never worried me. Then I saw *Patton*, the popular motion picture. In the movie was a scene where General Patton was addressing his troops in a very colorful manner. During his speech, Patton made a statement that stuck in my mind, never to be forgotten. In fact, it changed my life. He said, "America loves a winner and will not tolerate a loser."

This statement blew my mind. All of a sudden, winning and losing became important to me. In fact, it worried me sick. I knew I had lost many times during my life, but I never dreamed it could be that devastating. And now, because I had lost, did America hate me? No, America didn't hate me for losing. But America does put emphasis on winning. The spotlight is always on the winner. If you don't agree, tell me the names of people who almost broke records, or the names of the four teams that Pittsburgh beat in the Superbowls, or show me the trophy for the second runnerup in the Heisman trophy, or better still, why does Sugar Ray Leonard, and not the boxers he beats, make 7-Up commercials?

It's true. America does love a winner! Therefore, we need to know the specific differences between *winners* and *losers*. President Theodore Roosevelt offers this explanation:

> Far better it is to dare mighty things, to win glorious triumphs even though checkered with failure, than to take rank with those poor spirits who neither enjoy much nor suffer much because they live in that grey twilight that knows not victory or defeat.

What Roosevelt is telling us is that if at first you don't succeed, try, try again. It's simple and it's true. But it wasn't until I experienced these words in real life, either personally or through a friend, that I caught the full vision.

A good friend of mine, Pete, was a track man at Monterey High School in California. He was a good athlete and established himself as a great triple jumper on the school team.

Before we proceed, and in order for you to understand this story, you need to know two things about track meets. First, in a track meet, the scoring of events is as follows: the athlete who takes first place receives three points for his team total; two points go to second place; one point goes to

63

the third place finisher. The team with the most points accumulated at the end of the meet wins.

The second thing you need to realize is that the triple jump, the event in which my friend Pete competed, comes at the very end of a track meet. I mean at the very end! The dogs are running around on the field, the stands are empty, the janitor is sweeping the track, and most everyone is already on the bus to go home.

At this one particular track meet, there weren't the usual minimum three athletes competing in the 220-yard dash. Therefore, the track coach came up to Pete and asked him if he would run the race just to pick up the one point for third place which would help out the team score. All Pete would have to do is finish and his team would have the one point. The triple jump wouldn't be starting for a while, so Pete would still have time to rest and stretch before his event. He agreed to do it.

When the time came for the race, Pete got down in the blocks and the gun went off. Of course, the two awesome speedsters shot out of the blocks, down the straight, and were around the curve before Pete even got started. But that was all right; Pete only needed to come in third to win the point for his team.

As the runners were coming around the final curve, Pete heard some footsteps closing in on him from behind. What, had another sprinter entered the race? How can this be? he thought. With all of the people around the track, Pete had failed to notice him at the start of the race. Now what was he going to do? This wasn't part of the bargain! Thoughts started racing across his mind. He didn't want to be embarrassed and lose. He didn't want to take last place and miss picking up the point for his team. He didn't want people to laugh at him. So — he quit! With the race nearly over, he stopped right in the middle of the track and jogged off into the infield. Before I draw a conclusion from this story, I want to take you to Pete's next track meet one week later.

Pete's coach heard through the grapevine that there was only one hurdler on the opposing school's track team. So he asked Pete again if he would train for the hurdles during the week and run them on Friday just to pick up the one point awarded for third place. Pete said that he would with one condition: that there were only two other guys in the race. If there were three or more, he would not run the hurdles. He didn't want to lose and be humiliated again in front of all his friends.

Friday came and when the announcement of the hurdles event came over the loudspeaker, Pete walked to the starting blocks to check things out. There were three men getting ready to run so Pete decided not to compete. Remember, he did not want to be humiliated again. When the gun went off, one hurdler was great and flew out of the blocks over the hurdles and on to victory. But the other guys looked like total spastics. One was jumping over the hurdles sideways, and the other was knocking them all down. They were tripping and falling over each other. They didn't have a clue to what they were doing, and they made total fools of themselves. But one picked up the two points for second place and the other picked up the one point for third place.

Now, after hearing about both track meets and both experiences that Pete had, what can we conclude about winners and losers?

If you begin a race and quit before it is over for fear of losing or humiliation and embarrassment, or if you decide not to enter the race at all because you are too scared to compete, then you are the biggest loser of them all. You lose in both cases.

What about winning? Winning doesn't always label the guy at the top of the pile when the struggle is over. Winning goes a lot deeper than that.

Vince Lombardi, the great football coach of the Green Bay Packers, at the end of an important championship game where his team was defeated, started grabbing his players by their jerseys and shaking them off their chairs. All of them were hanging their heads. Some were crying, others were moping, all because of the great disappointment they were feeling. Lombardi couldn't take it any longer. He yelled at each one of them until he had their individual, undivided attention. When it was quiet, he taught them one of the greatest two-line lessons in all recorded history. He said simply, "Men, today you didn't lose. Time ran out . . . but you didn't lose."

Here were these great athletes, these great professional football heroes who had given it everything they had but still had been defeated on the scoreboard. Were they losers? Of course they weren't losers! And the coach knew it.

Life is the same way. Lombardi's words were not only great counsel for his ball players, but they are also powerful guidelines for us in our everyday lives.

You see, each time two or more people compete against each other, there will always be one who comes out on top; one who scores more points than the other; one who wins the game. Every day half of all the tennis players in the world lose their matches. But does that make them losers? In every golf tournament, only one golfer ends up with the lowest score and wins the tourney. Does this mean that all of the other golfers are losers?

Winning Is All the Time

Of course not! Winning isn't a sometime thing, it's an all-the-time thing. You don't just win once in a while, you've got to win all the while. Winning isn't just on the scoreboard. It isn't measured merely in points, it's measured in *effort*. Winning is an attitude, a habit, a way of life. Winning is a commitment to excellence, a promise to yourself that no matter what the obstacles or tasks may be, you will overcome them and give the very best of your ability. Winning means you will do whatever is necessary to be the best you can be at any given moment. It's an understanding that even if you didn't win the specific point or the game, you know you did your very best and can still hold your head high. You realize private victories precede public victories and if your effort truly was your best, no one, including yourself, can expect any more.

How can we achieve and develop this winning attitude? How can we become winners? The process is simple.

If we take life instant by instant, moment by moment, always remembering that we cannot live more than one second at a time, we will be successful — we will be champions. If we concentrate on being the best we can be right now and don't worry about the past or the future, we will be winners. The past is gone, why worry about it? We can't change or alter it. And the future has not yet come; we can't live in a dreamland. The only way we will ever become winners is to fully live each specific moment. By so doing, we eliminate from our lives the worst thing that can happen to us: experiencing the sick feeling of looking back on some instant in our lives that didn't turn out like we hoped and saying to ourselves, "If only I had done this, I could have been All-State," or "If I had done this right, I could have made the school play." The next time you need to make an important decision, remember the phrase, "Live life as though each day, each second, was your last."

To add to our already long list of interpretations of winning and losing, ask yourself: Of the following definitions, which ones apply to me?

— A winner is one who welcomes opposition and who views his problems as challenges and opportunities.

— A loser runs from opposition and problems.

— A winner single-shots with a long-barreled rifle.

— A loser blasts away with a sawed-off shotgun.

— A winner always learns something positive and grows from his mistakes.

— A loser learns that he doesn't want to take a chance on making a mistake, so he never tries anything new, challenging, or different.

— A winner believes opportunity doesn't knock, but must be created. He determines what happens to him by what he does or fails to do.

— A loser believe in fate. "Whatever happens, happens —I have no choice."

A winner is the sum total of the "winner" statements above, and from them we can see what a winner is and what he does. But there is another part of winning: What causes a person to do all this? What makes him victorious? Many have endured agony and pain and have overcome un-believable obstacles to perform incredible, almost impossible tasks. What is this force that makes them win?

Desire

To some, this inner power is referred to as "second effort" or "sticktoitiveness"; others refer to it as "intestinal fortitude" or just plain "guts." All of these definitions are good, but there is another word that totally captures the meaning of this amazing power within us — *desire*.

What makes a person give it everything they've got when less would be sufficient? *Desire*. What makes someone finish everything he starts? *Desire*. What makes someone practice day in and day out until he becomes the very best he can possibly be? *Desire*.

Desire is an extraordinary, intense determination that is above and beyond all other determinations. It is a fighting heart with a burning commitment to a cause. Let me dramatize what I mean.

I believe that there is more to athletic competition than just muscle and bone going through motion. It's more than a world of anatomy. It's a world of struggle, fierce determination, and deep desire. Sports competition is life personified. In fact, to be successful in life, you must think like a sports champion thinks. You see, sports champions believe they can run faster, jump higher, and throw farther than ever before. That's why they continue to break world records. They understand desire and are willing to "go for it" regardless of the situation.

In 1975 during the U.S. Open Tennis Championships, I witnessed one of the greatest exhibitions of desire in sports competition history. It involved a young tennis star from Spain, Manuel Orantes.

Orantes had been playing several tournaments during the course of the year and had established himself as one of the best players in the world. But for some reason, this U.S. Open Tennis Tournament was different. No matter how hard he tried, the ball just didn't bounce well in his court. It was one of those tournaments where nothing seemed to be going his way.

It didn't bother him, though. Being the great competitor that he is, Manuel never gave up and battled his way through each match. As hard and discouraging as it was, he continued to persevere one shot at a time through this long streak of bad luck. It finally paid off when he worked his way through the qualifying matches and ended up as one of the final four players. Orantes now would play the famous tennis star, Guillermo Vilas.

As the match began, Manuel's confidence was once again

renewed and he thought for sure that he could win. But contrary to his desire and belief, his string of bad luck continued. The winner of this match had to win three of five sets to advance to the finals. And before Orantes could even get untracked, he found himself behind two sets to none, five games to none, 5 to 40 in Vilas' favor, with Vilas serving. In other words, Vilas was killing him! It was the final set, the final game of the set, and the final point of the match. All Vilas had to do was win this one last point and he would win the match and advance to the finals.

In all reality and according to the best oddsmakers in the world, there was no believable way that Orantes could win. He was just too far behind. But did he believe this? No — Manuel Orantes is a champion. He is a winner and winners never give up.

Orantes started by winning the critical point and came back to win the semifinal match against Vilas. It was a grueling match lasting over five hours and ending at 1:30 a.m. Orantes had been totally worn out physically, mentally, and emotionally, and was theoretically too far behind to ever win. But he did!

Winning the semifinal match placed him in the finals and should have turned his luck in his favor. But it just wasn't to be. He was scheduled to play the top-ranked Jimmy Connors for the championship early the next day. Because Orantes hadn't had much sleep and because almost every ounce of energy had been drained from his body in winning against Vilas, the odds again were against him. Somehow, however, Orantes found the strength to walk out onto the court and once again gave it his very best effort. As the underdog and with everything going against him — his bad luck streak, his energy level, the lack of sleep he had the night before, the blisters on the bottom of his feet, his sore and tired hand, and his dramatic comeback the night before which had weakened him emotionally — how could he possibly rise to another occasion so soon? On the other hand, Jimmy Connors had had a good night's sleep and a whole day of rest going into this final match. It just didn't seem fair!

But Manuel Orantes beat Jimmy Connors in straight sets, 6-4, 6-3, 6-3. In an interview after the match, Orantes was asked how he did it — what was his strategy? He replied, "When I walked out onto the court, I knew exactly what had to be done and I knew that I didn't have the time or energy to 'dink around' with Connors. If I was going to win, I was going to have to put him away as quickly as possible and beat him three sets to nothing. If I was going to win, it would be because of my desire."

What a great champion! He never gave up. He won because he believed that he could do it. It would have been easy for Orantes to give up and concede defeat when he was so far behind against Vilas, but he didn't. It would have been easy for him to say that he was too tired to play against Connors, but he didn't. He was a true winner in every sense of the word. He wanted to win, was willing to win, and therefore he did win.

This story is a beautiful explanation of why winners and champions are great individuals. Remember, they're just average people like you and me, but they're great in that they always give an above-average effort to their challenges. That is their secret. Winners don't just dream and talk about winning, they *do* it. This brings me to an interesting point.

If being a champion and winning is really this easy, why do so many people very seldom win? Why do most individuals just remain average? Think about it.

An "Average" Person

And while you are thinking about your average day and the average effort you put forth toward accomplishing average things in your life, let me tell you about someone else who also does just average work. She is an average girl with average hobbies and interests, born to a typically average family. She paints a little, embroiders a little, has made a bead necklace and knitted a sweater. She can type a little, sew a little, and even has pretty writing. You know, the basic "run of the mill" talents that most average girls have. But — is she really just average?

This "average" girl's name is Elaine Dart. She is a cerebral palsy victim and has absolutely no use of her arms. Consequently Elaine has done all of these things that you and I take for granted with her toes. It took her two years to paint a picture of the Last Supper in oils; six months more to embroider a picture of the same scene; two years to knit a sweater that was presented to Jacqueline Kennedy Onassis when she was in the White House; and several months to string a one-thousand bead necklace. She can type a sheet of paper in several minutes, write beautifully with a pen, and thread a needle in eighteen seconds — all with her toes. And Elaine puts forth this extraordinary amount of effort just to be average like you and me. Think about what would happen to her as a handicapped person if she put forth only an average amount of effort, the same amount of effort that many of us put forth in our lives. She wouldn't accomplish anything and would be an average handicapped individual.

I want you to compare your own individual effort to Elaine's individual effort. How do you match up? I bet most of you have never given this much effort toward anything in your whole life. What would happen if you did?

Think about what you could accomplish if you were to put forth the same amount of effort that Elaine puts forth to bring herself up to what is average for most people. The answer is again obvious. The sky is the limit if you understand that things don't just happen, but you *make* them happen. You see, a champion is an average person who gives an above-average effort to make things happen. And the best part about this is that anyone — yes, even you and me — can do that in any field we're interested in.

Elaine Dart is a true champion, a total winner in every sense of the word. She is a living monument of proof that you can't keep a winner down, that you can't hold back a champion. Somehow, no matter what happens, a champion always manages to keep going. A winner always transforms bad times into good and never makes excuses.

The Los Angeles Lakers and the Philadelphia 76ers were battling it out in a seven-game NBA championship tournament. In the sixth game in Los Angeles, the Lakers lost, forcing the title game to be played in Philadelphia. Also in the sixth game, Kareem Abdul-Jabbar, the big 7'2" center for L.A., suffered a detached retina, injuring his eye so severely that he couldn't make the trip with his team to Philadelphia for the last game.

71

This was a devastating blow to the Lakers, and most thought it nullified their chances of winning the championship.

So what did Los Angeles do? They had every reason and opportunity to make excuses for probably losing, but did they use them? No — because the Lakers are winners.

What they did was take a twenty-one-year-old rookie, barely out of his sophomore year in college, who was only a 6'8" guard, and move him to center to replace Jabbar. And if that wasn't shocking enough, he had to play against 6'11", 260-pound Darryl Dawkins, who smashes backboards and many new, inexperienced centers as part of his game.

Who was this youngster— this winner who scored 42 points that night to lead Los Angeles to the NBA championship title? Who was this winner who appropriately was awarded the Most Valuable Player trophy after the game? It was "Magic" Johnson. And believe me, if you saw the game as I did, you'd agree they named him right!

As you've been reading these stories, perhaps you've said to yourself, "Sure, these people are champions; they were born with exceptional abilities, and I have to agree some are born with more natural talent than others. But talent alone is no guarantee of success." I understand when you say, "Why even try? I'm never going to be any good anyway. The same people always win at everything." But don't worry. I want you to know that you are not alone. Many feel this way. The secret, though, is knowing you don't have to stay this way.

Remember that the same people who keep winning time after time don't *always* have to win. These constant winners have not always been winners. They, too, began as average individuals. But through desire and constant effort, they managed to become the best they could be and become perennial champions.

When I was playing football at the University of Utah, I learned something very important about average people becoming winners that proved this fact to me: the same people don't always have to win.

Think Like Champions!

It was my sophomore year, the third game of the football season, and we were playing UCLA. They were ranked in the top ten teams nationally and had for their quarterback a Heisman Trophy candidate. In fact, UCLA was so big and awesome that this particular year their offensive line weight averaged more than the Los Angeles Ram's line. To top it off, their running backs were bigger and faster than I was, and I played defensive end!

In contrast to them, here we were, the University of Utah. We had lost our first two games, one to the last-place team in the league, and one to Oregon State. We were small in size and inexperienced, and we had a brand-new coaching staff. In other words, we were the underdogs and no one, not even our mothers, gave us a chance of beating mighty UCLA.

Game time finally came and we took the field as usual for pre-game drills. They were the same as they had always been, right up to the side straddle hops. And then it happened — in a sudden thundering stampede of feet, the UCLA team came out of the locker room, turned the corner onto the field in a slow, confident, cocky jog, and lined up for calisthenics. We all took a good look — each one of them was huge and ornery looking! And the worst part about it was that they were all staring and smiling at us as if they were going to eat us for dinner.

I have to admit, and I wasn't the only one swallowing hard and shaking, that we were nervous and definitely intimidated by the sight of that team. But still things weren't too bad because they were clear over on the far side of the field and we seemed fairly safe. Then suddenly, one UCLA player overthrew a warmup pass and a teammate came over to get the ball. As this guy got closer and closer he kept getting bigger and bigger until he looked at least eight feet twenty inches tall — and that was when he bent over to pick up the ball! I mean he was one big old dude!

Pre-game warmups mercifully ended and we hurried off the field to the safety of the locker room. As the coaches filed in one at a time, we could tell they sensed something was wrong with our team. As we sat there on the benches, big-eyed and very quiet, our linebacker coach stepped forward and gave one of the greatest speeches I've ever heard. He stood there with his hat turned backwards and in his deep, slow voice he said, "Men, you're all scared! You're acting like a bunch of sissies! I sense a little nervousness in you tonight. But why? Why are you scared? What do you have to be afraid of? There is no reason to be nervous. UCLA is not better than you. They put on shoes just like you do. They put on pants, shoulder pads, and helmets just like you do. They're no better than you are. In fact, they don't know what they're in for! We're going to beat them! I don't care if they are UCLA or even the Dallas Cowboys for that matter. They don't always have to win! It's our turn tonight! We are going to win! Go out and drill 'em!"

In a matter of seconds, the University of Utah Utes were transformed from scared little boys into mighty warriors. And what brought about this change in us? We now believed we *could* beat the Bruins. It didn't matter how big and strong or how fast they were; it didn't matter that they were supposed to win by forty points. We didn't care that the newspapers gave us one chance in a billion to win. We just didn't care.

But then the game started, and oh, baby, was it a doosey! We got the ball first — and they took it right away. Now it was our turn to stop them. As I jogged out onto the field to take my spot at the defensive end slot, I had to admit it was hard for me to believe the coach's words, especially when UCLA came up to the line of scrimmage. When the tight end lined up in front of me, I couldn't see anything else. He was a moose! My job as defensive end was to react to something called the "triangle technique." I had to look at the quarterback, locate the nearest running back, and watch the tight end in front of me. They formed a triangle and what they did determined where I would go. I had to keep my eye on all of them.

So how was I supposed to do that when I couldn't see anybody? The guy in front of me was so big I had to look through his legs to see the quarterback! As I was doing so, and before I could adjust, the quarterback barked the signals and they hiked the ball. As I stepped across the line totally off balance to stop their famous "veer-option," I suddenly saw a blur out of the corner of my eye. The next thing I remembered was flying through the air, landing on my back, and hearing the roar of fans shooting through my ears as I lay on my back about ten feet from where I had been. Obviously, when I heard people cheering and laughing, I thought someone had scored, so I wobbled up to my knees and turned to see if there was someone in the end zone. As I looked up, no one was there but something else was wrong. It was one of the weirdest sensations I'd ever had. It was as though I was looking through a telescope, like I had tunnel vision. But what had really happened was — remember that blur I had seen out of the corner of my eye? Well, he was 6'7" and 285 pounds. I mean this guy could have kick-started a 747 jet! He hit me so hard that he broke my chin strap, bent my face mask, and twisted my helmet around on my head so that I was looking out the ear hole! There I knelt with the crowd oohing and aahing because this turkey had "cleaned my clock." As I tried to get up, the guy was still standing over me, laughing, with his arms straight in the air. Finally, when he moved, I struggled to my feet, broke into tears because I hurt so bad, and waddled off the field to rearrange my face, fix my nose, and straighten my broken helmet. As I sat there for a couple of plays, with my mouth bleeding, I kept remembering the coach's words, "The same people don't always have to win. UCLA is not any better than you. Tonight's our turn to win." As these words continued to ring through my ears, I couldn't help but think, He must be joking. How would he like to get his bell rung by a three hundred-pound gorilla? Who was he fooling? The only chance we had of winning was if I ran down to the end of the field, loaded the cannon they shot off on kickoffs with real bullets, hid behind it, and shot it off on every play.

Well, my helmet and my face were finally fixed and I reluctantly went back into the game. I didn't want to play — believe me! As far as I was concerned I had quit — but the coach didn't seem to understand that, so he sent me back in. But do you know what? On the very next play we sacked the quarterback and caused a fumble on the option that we recovered. Hey, things were looking up! Our offense came out and immediately scored. On the next defensive series we snuffed them again and recovered their fumble. We scored again. The next time they got the ball, we drilled the quarterback again and again. He thought he was caught in a revolving door —it was great! We caused another fumble that we recovered, and we scored again! Things were really looking up now. Maybe the coach was right. Maybe the same folks don't always have to win. This belief got stronger as we kept drilling them — "That's right, we're bad" — and the halftime score proved it — Utah 19, UCLA 0. We were beating UCLA at their own game, not necessarily physically, but mentally and emotionally.

"Great!" you say. "But what was the final score?" Before I conclude this story you must understand what I'm trying to tell you. I know the same people don't always have to win, as I played in numerous games when my team was the underdog and we won. We came from behind to beat Arizona State. We also came back from a 27-0 deficit against Arizona to win at the buzzer, and we completed a fourth down and twenty yards to go pass play to come from behind and beat conference champion BYU on the last play, 23-22! The underdog win list goes on and on; the same people or teams definitely don't always have to win! However, I chose to relate this UCLA experience because it not only demonstrates this point, but also puts across another crucial part of winning. Now the conclusion.

The second half was a little different. We were still ahead as the clock wound down, but then UCLA scored twice in a row on two big plays to beat us, 23-19. I realize it seems to defeat the purpose of telling this story when you know the ending, but the end of this story answers an important question: Why did UCLA win? Why is it that they who win usually always win when in fact they don't have to?

The reason that Utah lost that day and UCLA won is because somewhere toward the end of the game our team began to think, Hey, we're not supposed to be doing this. We are not supposed to be beating UCLA. We started to doubt ourselves. Consequently, because we believed that we weren't supposed to win the game, we let down mentally and eventually lost the game.

On the other hand, the reason UCLA or other winners

are able to win is because it comes natural. Winning is a habit with them. They have won for so long that they don't know how to do anything else. They have worked too long and too hard to lose, and they refuse to settle for anything but victory.

If you feel you aren't winning when you should, take a close look at yourself. Evaluate what you are going and list where you are winning and losing. Determine what is making the difference, then make the necessary changes and start making winning a habit.

As you make this list, remember something we've already discussed. A desire to win must be a habit. It has to be part of your personality and part of everything you do. You must remember that winning isn't a sometime thing but an all-the-time thing.

Make New Habits to Win

Habits of winning, just like any other habit, are learned. You can change from losing to winning simply by making new habits. These habits are what determine our destiny. "Sow a thought, reap an action; sow an action, reap a habit; sow a habit, reap a character; sow a character, reap a destiny."

If you want a very simple way to become a habitual winner, think back in your life to a specific moment when you did something that excited you, when you felt wanted and important, when you won and you felt like a million bucks. Try to remember those feelings you had while you were winning. If you can relive that experience and remember the great feelings you had when you did win, you can make winning a habit. Just begin by overcoming the four areas of "why you can't always do it" explained in the next chapter and start duplicating the emotions of winning as often as you can. If you have had great feelings once, you surely can have them again. And as you repeat this process and improve your technique from win to win, winning soon becomes a habit for you. From then on you'll work so hard at what you do that you'll never surrender until you win.

You see, you don't have to be a loser. You don't have to be poor. You don't have to live in a ghetto or be on welfare or drive an old, beat-up car or go hungry if you don't want to. You don't have to get Cs and Ds on your report card. You don't have to play second or third string on the team. Winning is a choice. We are in control. We decide our destiny. Winning can be summed up as follows: "Losers let it happen — winners make it happen." Think about this as you contemplate your dreams of enjoying the price of success. Then memorize Vince Lombardi's words:

"I firmly believe that any man's finest hour — his greatest fulfillment of all he holds dear — is that moment when he has worked his heart out in a good cause and lies exhausted on the field of battle — victorious."

Remember, you were born to succeed. You can become a champion! You can always win and be the best you can be! Now go out and do it!

Chapter Six

"Why Can't I Always Do It?"

How to Succeed Again and Again

The famous artist James Whistler once painted a tiny picture of a beautiful bouquet of flowers. The craftsmanship and pure artistry were outstanding. In fact, never before had man been able to capture so perfectly the beauty of nature. Every artist who saw the painting envied it and every collector yearned to buy it for his own. But regardless of the offer, the painter refused to sell. Why?

"Whenever I feel my hand has lost its touch," he replied, "whenever I doubt my ability, I go to the wall where this picture of the flowers is hanging and say to myself, 'You painted that. Your mind conceived the beautiful colors. Your steady hand drew it. Your graceful skill put the flowers on the canvas.' Then," he concluded, "I know that what I have done once I can definitely do again."

This famous artist then left us with his law of success: "Hang on the walls of your mind the memory and recollection of your successes. Take counsel of your strengths, not your weaknesses. Think of the magnificent jobs you have done. Think of the specific times when you rose above your average level of performance and became great for even an instant as you worked toward a dream for which you had deeply yearned. Then, as I have done, visit

Hang on the Walls of your Mind

the Memories of your Success

the walls of your mind on which these pictures of success are hanging and remember them as you travel the roads of life."

Whenever success is remembered in this way, the memory of what happened is increased. If you've done something successful once, you can surely do it again!

This is an important principle of life and must be remembered as you begin this chapter, for this chapter teaches you can do it, and it's true — you can.

How many times in your life have you heard the words, "You can do it!" It may be when you're still considering whether or not you even want to attempt the task, or it may come during a football play, a musical recital, a dance concert, or a math test. But regardless of the time, someone is always there to tell you, "You can do it!"

Why Can't I Do It?

If you can recall such an instance, I want you to look back on the outcome. Did you, in fact, do it? You were told you *could* do it, but were you always *able* to do it? If not, why not?

There are four simple reasons why.

1. I was afraid to try for fear of failure.
2. I didn't know exactly what it was that I wanted to do.
3. I didn't want to do it badly enough.
4. I didn't believe I really could do it.

Fear of Failure

Let's discuss each of these four reasons. First, fear of failure. In Chapter 4 we learned how to overcome fear, but now we need to discuss why we should. How many times have you decided not to enter the race, play the game, run for office, or try out for the play, club, or team just because you were afraid you wouldn't be chosen?

How many times have you clammed up or said no when an opportunity came your way, just because you were afraid to fail? I'm sure it's happened many times in your life; it has in mine. And you probably feel justified in saying no because you don't want to fail. But stop and think about it — failing is nothing to fear! We have all failed at one time or another, whether we want to admit it or not. Harry J. Gray has written:

> You've failed many times, although you may not remember. You fell down the first time you tried to walk. You almost drowned the first time you tried to swim. Did you hit the ball the first time you swung the bat? Heavy hitters, the ones who hit the most home runs, also strike out a lot. Babe Ruth struck out 1,330 times, but he also hit 714 home runs. R.H. Macy failed seven times before his store in New York caught on. English novelist John Creasey received 753 rejection slips before he published 564 books. See! Don't worry about failure. Worry about the chances you miss when you don't even try.

Robert Schuller said, "It's better to attempt something great and fail than to attempt nothing at all and succeed." Think about it. Isn't this the formula for success? On the wall of the Utah State Office of Education hangs this motto: "Most people are so afraid of failure that they are afraid to risk success. Yet the great law of growth is to try, fail, adjust, and try again. How does a bird learn to fly? How does a person become great?" The answer is always the same: Through hard work. Through trial and error. Through attempting something great and failing, falling, and getting up to try again. We must remember that for every adversity in life there is a seed of equivalent or greater benefit, and we must look for that seed.

Nothing in life needs to be feared; it needs only to be understood. If you have a positive attitude toward whatever you fear, eventually you will understand and overcome that fear. The quickest way to acquire this understanding and the self-confidence that follows is to do exactly what you are afraid to do. All failures and problems become smaller if you refuse to dodge them. Instead, confront them head on. "If you touch a thistle timidly it will prick you; grasp it boldly and its spines crumble." This is what we must do if we are going to crush the fear of failure in our lives.

You Can Win

> How do you tackle your work each day?
> Do you grapple the task that comes your way
>   With a confident, easy mind?
> Do you start to toil with a sense of dread
>   Or feel that you're falling behind?

> You can do as much as you think you can.
>   But you'll never accomplish more.
> If you're afraid of yourself, young man,
>   There's little for you in store.
> The failure comes from the inside first.
>   It's there, if we only knew it.
> And you can win, though you fear the worst,
>   If you feel that you're going to do it.
>
> Edgar A. Guest

In a scene from the movie *Rocky III*, Rocky is afraid of losing an important fight and is being lectured by his wife. He has already been beaten badly and has lost his heavyweight championship; he is scheduled to fight this man again and is truly afraid. The following conversation is paraphrased from the movie dialogue.

Adrian: You've never quit anything before. Why now?

Rocky: Because before, in all the other fights, I thought I was something. I thought I was good. I thought I was a champion. Mickey [the former trainer] didn't have to lie to me and make me feel I was better than I was when I wasn't. The fighters were hand-picked. Nothing was real! You see, Mickey was just trying to protect me but it only made things worse. I've gone three years thinking I was a winner, but I'm not. I'm really a loser! So what if I had the title for so long? I don't believe in myself anymore! And when you don't believe in yourself anymore, you're finished — through — that's it. Now, for the first time in my life, I want to quit. I'm afraid, Adrian, I'm afraid!

Adrian: I'm afraid, too! But there's nothing wrong with being afraid! You're human, aren't you? You have no right to feel guilty for what happened. You were a champion and you did what you were expected to do. You did what I and everybody else thought you should do! And now you're trying to tell me these fighters weren't real? Well, I don't believe it! But it doesn't matter what I believe, because you're the one who has to carry that fear around inside you. Afraid that everybody is going to take things away! Afraid you're going to be remembered as a coward! That you're not a man anymore! Well, it's not true! But it doesn't matter what I think, because you're the one who has to settle it. And you've got to overcome the fear now, or it will bother you for the rest of your life. Look what it's done to you

83

already! No matter how hard it might be, you've got to fight. Apollo [the new trainer] thinks you can do it and I think you can do it, but you've got to want to do it for the right reasons. Not for me, not for anybody! Not for the title, for money, or for those who chant your name, but for yourself! For you, and for you alone!

Rocky: And if I lose?

Adrian: Then you lose! At least you lose with no excuses — with no fear! You lose with your head high, knowing you gave it your very best shot. And no one ever needs to be ashamed of that.

Before we conclude this section, let's discuss one final point about fear. If you're anything like me, I'm sure you're impatient for success. By this I mean you want things right now. You don't want to have to wait for success. You want things to go right the first time with no trials and errors.

Knowing that disappointments and pitfalls can happen is one of the foremost causes of fear. This is why we tend not to try very hard at tasks we're afraid of failing in, for we know if we fail while giving it our best effort, we leave ourselves with no excuses if things don't work out as planned. And if we allow this fear to continue, it will eventually block our ambition altogether. Then we're finished; we'll never want to try again.

Hey, if you are like this, recognize this hangup and stop it before it ruins you! We cannot afford to use fear as an excuse. We need to stop being afraid of failure and realize that success is not an event but a means to an end. Success is not a destination but an up-and-down, trial-and-error journey to the top. Success is never found at the top of the hill if duties at the bottom are neglected. And these duties take time, seasoning, and hard work.

Success takes practice! It's the place in the road where preparation, which eliminates fear, and opportunity meet. Few people recognize success, though, because too often it comes disguised as hard work. And we all know hard work involves hardship, failure, and sometimes defeat.

The solution, then, to the first reason for "why I can't do it " is simply overcoming the fear of hard work, for when you overcome this fear, you overcome the fear of failure. Regardless of the difficulty of the task or uncertainty of the future, if you hang in there long enough, hard work will prevail and eliminate your fear of failure. Remember, the harder you work for something, the harder it is to surrender. And if you refuse to surrender, you'll eventually become successful.

The next time you're afraid to fail, or afraid of what others may say, realize there's nothing to fear but fear itself. Just dig in, work hard, and remember Theodore Roosevelt's words:

> In the battle of life, it is not the critic who counts, not the man who points out how the strong man stumbled or how the doer of the deed could have done better; the credit belongs to the man who is actually in the arena; whose face is marred by dust and sweat and blood; who strives valiantly; who errs and comes short again and again because there is no effort without error and shortcomings; who does actually strive to do the deeds; who knows the great enthusiasms and the great devotions, and spends himself in a worthy cause; who, at the best, knows in the end the triumph of high achievement; and who, at the worst, if he fails, at least fails while daring greatly; so that his place shall never be with those timid souls who have never tasted neither victory nor defeat.

This brings us to the second reason why "I can't do it": "I didn't know exactly what I wanted to do."

Know What You Want to Do

Do you sometimes feel like you don't know where you're going or what you want to do? Have you ever felt like a pop can in the ocean, tossed around, bobbing to and fro, and carried by the wind to wherever it takes you? And the longer you continue floating through life with no direction, the more frustrated you become.

If you have, I want you to know that you're not alone. It's not out of the ordinary to wonder what you want to do; all of us go through it. But the key to your happiness in life is for you to overcome these feelings of frustration, uncertainty, and doubt as soon as possible. For the sooner you know where you're going, the faster you'll be able to get there.

Many young people seem to think they're too young to decide what they want to do or where they want to go. They feel there's plenty of time to procrastinate today and decide on a career later. I hope you're not one of these procrastinators, for it is between the ages of twelve and twenty-two that we make most of the major decisions in our lives. The decisions you make during these years will affect you for the rest of your life. Think about it!

You may be sitting there saying to yourself, "Hey, I'm only twelve years old. How in the world can what I decide to do today affect my whole life?" Or maybe you're a big high school hard guy who thinks to himself, "Hey, I'm gonna just keep on cruisin' for a while — there's always time later to pull my head out and change and do what I really want to do. I don't need to make important decisions now."

. I want you to think about the decisions you're now faced with. For example, right now you're choosing and developing life-long friends who should have the same ideals, motivations, and goals that you have. You're making decisions about health habits and moral codes. You're wondering about religious and philosophical directions. You're forming views about drugs, tobacco, alcohol, and sex. If you still fail to see the urgency of making these decisions early, think about this for a moment: Statistics show many kids who are convicted felons at thirteen, bona fide alcoholics at fourteen, and hard drug addicts at fifteen. And can you imagine what it would be like to be a father or have a baby when you're only in the seventh grade? I just met a girl who was illegitimately pregnant for the second time, and she was only sixteen! This is sad!

Another major decision that you'll have to make between the ages of twelve and twenty-two is that of your education. Are you going to stick it out and graduate from high school? I hope you realize the extreme importance of this one! Are you going on to trade tech, college, or a major university? If so, you must decide today to be a hardworking student and realize that your grades must be good and your study habits sound. If you want to be an NCAA athlete you have to have good grades. There are too many outstanding players with good grades for a college to want to recruit someone who is flunking out.

The list continues. You've got to decide on your occupation. What are you going to do to provide a good living for you and your future family? You've got to decide about the military — will you or won't you join? These are a few of the many decisions you have to make while you're young and still in school. Now is the time to decide who and what you want to be.

Now I don't expect that you'll simply be able to stop, change, and make all the proper decisions at once. Therefore, here is a little exercise I want you to try. The next time you're faced with a major decision and you want to make sure it will take you to where you want to be in life, I want you to do something to demonstrate the importance of knowing where you want to go and finding out how to get there. It will also show how making one right decision early can steer you in the proper direction to accomplish the desired result. I want you to go to a bowling alley or a golf course, sign up, pay your money, and play. Analyze every part of your game and relate it to your life. What you do when you're bowling or playing golf is exactly what you should do in life. For example, you have an alley or a fairway in front of you that tells you specifically the direction you must go in order to accomplish what you want to do. This helps put you on the right track. Then when you step up to roll or hit the ball, you see your goal — ten pins to knock down or a hole on a green many yards away to knock the ball into. After you have rolled or hit the ball, you're on your way to accomplishing what you set out to do.

The next step is easier. You still know where you're going and what needs to be done to get there, but this time you only have four pins to knock down or two putts to put the ball into the cup. As you continue with your game, you'll notice that each time you finish one accomplishment, it's time to move to the next, and so forth, until you have finished what you set out to do. The end result is ten frames or eighteen holes with the best score possible.

You see, playing golf or bowling is like playing the game of life. When you decide what you want to do, and continue to plug away at it one decision at a time, life becomes more simple, you stop wasting time, and you eventually get there. The key is knowing what *you* want to do.

If you want something because others are doing it, or because someone is telling you you should do it, you'll only go through the motions with a half-hearted effort and seldom be able to do it.

You, therefore, need to not only know *what* you want to do, but also *why* you want to do it. This is where motivation comes in — not false motivation that comes from others trying to get you excited, but self-motivation. Without this knowledge of why, there will be no value in doing, we won't give it our best effort, and most likely the job won't get done.

What I'm getting at is that motivation has to be *self-*motivation. It has to come from within, not from without. And when it does, you'll not only know what you want to do, but you'll also be able to say "I want to" instead of "I have to" or "I'm supposed to" which will insure your success in getting it done.

You've Got to Want It

The third answer to "Why can't I do it?" is "I didn't want to do it badly enough." The choice to succeed is definitely a choice. It's your choice! People who succeed in life decide they want to badly enough, and they do. Because this is true, we also need to realize the opposite is true. Those who fail choose to fail. They don't want to succeed badly enough.

You see, there is a difference between wanting to do something and wanting to do it badly enough. Wanting to do something is going to get you on the football field, into the music hall or dance studio, or into the math class; it will get you to the point of going through the motions; but it will never get you to the point of winning, of excellence, of success. My father taught me a great principle when he said, "Anything worth doing is worth doing right." Why do something just to be doing it? We must not confuse activity with accomplishment. If something is worth doing, don't fool around with it — do it! And do it to the very best of your ability! You can't just want it, you have to want it badly enough. Wanting to win is only of the mind. But wanting to win badly enough takes this wish of the mind and puts it alongside a burning desire of the heart. Together they can help you do anything. Wanting to win badly enough means you will sweat, toil, struggle, kick, and scratch to get what you want.

There's an old and popular story told about the great philosopher, Aristotle. A young man came to him one day and asked Aristotle to give him all the knowledge and learning he possessed. He wanted Aristotle to teach him everything he knew. Aristotle said he would consider it, but first he wanted to take the young lad for a walk down by the river. When they arrived at the riverbank, Aristotle threw a stone into the river and asked the boy to pick it up for him. When the lad stooped over and leaned toward the river, Aristotle grabbed him and dunked his head under the cold water. He held it under and kept it there for quite a while until the young man began to swing his arms, kick his feet, struggle and squirm, and fight for his freedom. He needed air! The lad wanted to live and he wanted air badly enough that he was willing to do anything to get it.

After the lesson was sufficiently taught, Aristotle let the boy up for air. After he caught his breath, and was once again able to speak, the lad asked, "Hey, what did you do that for?" Aristotle replied, "I will give you and teach you all that I know, but it will do you no good unless you want it badly enough — unless you want it as much as you wanted air to breathe."

This is what I mean when I say you've got to want it badly enough. Whatever you want must be wanted so much that you'd do anything to get it.

OK, you've got to want it badly enough, but you ask, "Want what? What should I want?" The answer is, you should want to win!

The great football coach Vince Lombardi is often misquoted as saying, "Winning isn't everything, it's the only thing." What he really said was, "Winning isn't everything; wanting to win is everything."

What does wanting to win mean? It's where winning begins. If you want to win, it means you are willing to do everything in your power to win, to achieve, to be successful. Wanting to win starts in the mind. It starts as a thought, a dream, then turns into a commitment, then into dedication and determination, and finally ends up as endurance to the end and reaching a goal.

I want to tell you three short stories about individuals who had extraordinary determination, who wanted to win badly enough, who learned how to exercise mind over matter, who overcame obstacles, and who became the best they could be.

The first story is about Laurie Mitchell. Recently I flew to Montana to speak at the Helena High School commencement exercises. After I had delivered my remarks, the diploma presentations began. Toward the middle of the presentation, as the students filed past one by one, I noticed a very young-looking girl walking up to receive her diploma. She appeared to be about twelve years old, and I figured she must be a genius who had finished high school early. When her diploma was presented to her, the crowd arose and gave her a standing ovation. This deeply moved me, so I asked the principal sitting next to me about her.

This beautiful little girl was Laurie Mitchell. Laurie was not twelve, as I had supposed, but eighteen years of age. She was graduating with her peers. Laurie was not a genius, but she was close to it. She graduated third in her class of 347, and was an honor student. This isn't so extraordinary, so what makes her story so special?

Laurie was born with numerous physical handicaps. Her right hand, the one she took and held her diploma with, has only a thumb. Her left arm extends only to the elbow. Laurie's right leg has no femur bone and she has no left leg at all. She walks on one artificial leg and has a brace on the other. Laurie stands only four feet two inches tall.

Laurie's condition is serious but she doesn't let it bother her. She doesn't concern herself so much with why she's the way she is as she does with how she will overcome her daily obstacles and become the best she can be. Laurie Mitchell truly wants to do it badly enough! You see, Laurie has courage, determination, and an exceptional ability to accept a challenge. She will never be labeled a quitter or a loser as she has the ability to turn the impossible into reality.

For example, at the age of six, she was determined to learn how to swin. Three months later and after long hours of practice, Laurie achieved her goal to the amazement of many. Today she is an excellent swimmer.

Living on a ranch exposed her to another goal she wanted to accomplish: learning to ride a horse. After several months of practice and with a specially designed saddle, she could sit on the horse and ride it, but she found that commanding the horse to move forward was a problem. This is usually accomplished by kicking the horse in the side or flanks. After trying many ways to get the horse to move, she finally found one that succeeded. Now after climbing up into her saddle, Laurie simply leans over and bites the horse's ear. Of course, the horse takes off at a dead run.

Laurie Mitchell continues to succeed and is now attending college, fulfilling a lifelong dream.

The second story is about a friend of mine, Bill Latimer. Bill is one of the greatest athletes in America. As a student at the University of Utah, he was a star on the tennis team and one of the awesome skiers in the Intermountain West. All was going well for Bill. Things couldn't be better.

One winter, however, a challenge came into Bill's life. It was the weekend of the Intermountain Gelande Ski Jumping Contest at Solitude, Utah. The top jumpers from the area were competing for points in form and distance. At the end of the contest, as is usually the case, they began the most spectacular ski jumping event, where the contestants try to outdo each other with breathtaking aerial somersaults, twists, and maneuvers. Being the competitive man that he is, Bill decided to go for the longest jump of the day. He wanted to "get the most air," not only to excite himself, but also to excite the crowd and take home a trophy.

I remember watching Bill hike way up into the trees until I could hardly see him. A blizzard set in, and he slipped completely out of sight. Suddenly, at the announcement of his name, out of the fog came Bill, skiing frantically, trying to get up as much speed as he possibly could. By the time he reached the jump, he was going about 50 miles an hour. When he hit the end of the jump, it was as though he'd been shot out of a cannon. He sailed up and up — I thought he'd never come down! As he flew through the air, he sailed way past the landing hill, traveling a distance of 215 feet, and landed on the flat, hard, icy snow. It was as though he'd fallen out of a fifty-foot-high building onto the sidewalk.

Because he hadn't expected such a long ride through the air, Bill found himself sitting back on his skis. When he landed, the back of his skis hit first and the tremendous impact pressure snapped his right leg off at the top of his boot. His foot was just dangling there, held together only by the skin. As the ski patrol attended to him, they found that his injury was more serious than a single broken bone in that he had broken his leg in the same place before. They rushed him to the nearest hospital, but his injuries were so severe that his leg had to be amputated just below the knee.

Can you imagine what this would feel like? One minute you're playing tournament tennis and skiing until the sun goes down; and the next minute you're waking up from surgery and finding your right leg missing. Needless to say, Bill was totally devastated!

But Bill got hold of himself, decided he "wanted it" badly enough, and made a commitment that day. He promised himself that he would never let anyone see him walk with a limp. He vowed that he would not let this accident stop him.

So Bill had two kinds of artificial legs made for him. One has a foot on it with a curved convex bottom. This has a rocking chair effect, and to this day, when he walks, he does not limp. No one knows he has an artificial leg unless he wears shorts. He still plays tournament tennis and beats some of the great ones in the Intermountain area. He is an amazing racquetball player. He swims, runs long distance races, and does all the things he used to do almost as well as he used to do them.

The other artificial leg he had made is constructed so that he can put a ski boot on it and ski. Bill is still a fantastic powder skier, but sometimes it's hard for him when he gets in the bumps. For example, one day when he was flying down the side of a mountain, he hit a big bump and his artificial leg flipped off and shot on down the mountain. Here it was, not just a ski flying down the hill, but a ski with a boot and a leg hooked on as well! Now picture this: below was a lady just trying to figure out how to ski, cruising back and forth across the mountain. When she looked up, she saw the ski coming down the hill and yelled "Ski! Ski!" to warn others. But as it got closer, she changed her scream to "No, it's a leg, it's a leg coming down the mountain!"

And to top it off, here came Bill skiing down the

mountain on one leg, chasing his other one. Finally the runaway leg stuck in the snow, stopping right in front of the lady, where Bill was able to catch up to it. What a sight! The lady was pale white, standing there in shock, with her wig on sideways, just staring at the leg as Bill brushed the snow from it, strapped it back on, and said, "It's okay, ma'am, it happens all the time."

Bill Latimer is a great man. He didn't stay down when he got knocked down and he didn't let obstacles and disappointments stop him. He overcame great barriers and succeeded as one who definitely can do it. In fact, I'm convinced he can do anything, because he is one who truly wants it badly enough.

This next story is about Glen Tenove, a man who has more determination and production power than anyone I've ever met or heard of. As I tell you a few of the countless competitive stories about him, remember that Tenove is supposed to be too small to play defensive end in college football. But he did it and was a star!

Tenove's story begins in his first semester at California State University at Long Beach, where he was an outstanding student athlete. In this first semester, Tenove enrolled in a conditioning class, where on the first day the instructor asked each student to perform nine different physical skills. Tenove finished in the top four in all of them. The instructor felt this was pretty good, but the next day Tenove came in and wanted to know the name of each person who had finished first in each category and what he looked like. He then watched them in class to see what they were doing, and stayed extra hours each night in the weight room to work out until the test at the end of the semester. When it came, he ended up first in seven tests and second in the other two, and, knowing how Tenove is, I'm sure he was angry about finishing second in any of them.

"I don't want to be good," says Tenove. "I want to be the best!" He seems miscast in a society in which potential is more highly prized than production.

"Potential, that's nothing," says Tenove. "People never use it. I don't know how much talent I have, but I do know I can beat people who have more talent because I refuse to lose to them."

Tenove has a notebook that spells out this deep belief. The inscription on it reads: "God, make it as tough as you like, but make it possible." This is from the book *Alive.* It's a story of a group of soccer players who survive a plane crash in the high Andes Mountains.

"Those guys were studs," Tenove says. "It took them seventy-three days to walk down off the mountain. They did it without snowshoes. They all lost at least fifty pounds, and they had to eat the people who died so that they could survive. The saying on my notebook was by one of the guys who climbed to the top of a mountain, thinking he had made it, only to realize there was another mountain. That's when he said, "God, make it as tough as you like, but make it possible." "That's the way I feel," he adds. "I don't care how tough it is; if it's possible, I'll make it!"

To most people, some of what Tenove does borders on the impossible. For example, he played the last three football games of his senior year with a separated shoulder. For the rest of the weekend following the injury, he worked at moving his arm until he could do it without reacting to the pain.

"After a while, you get used to the pain," he says. "It's like it isn't even there."

A few days after his injury he cheated on the examination to determine whether his shoulder was separated. In the examination, the doctor asked Tenove to hold weights in each hand. If his shoulder was separated, the weight would pull that arm down.

But, because Tenove had practiced moving his shoulder all weekend, he was able to withstand the pain, hold his arm in place using the muscles around the shoulder, and pass the test, even though his shoulder was separated.

"I didn't know how it was going to work," says Tenove, "but I thought it would, and it did. I knew if I couldn't lift that arm, I couldn't play any more. And there was no way I was going to have them tell me I couldn't play."

He reacted the same way to missing football practice. He was asked by his coach to not practice and rest his shoulder. But the frustration of missing practice was so great that at 11:30 at night, Tenove was seen running up and down the steps alongside the Student Union Building for more than an hour. He says, "I like to practice hard and go into a game a little bruised and beat up. I love to have the feeling that I've outworked everyone else."

Tenove's intensity isn't limited to just the football field. In the classroom he was a 3.75 student and a candidate for All-American academic honors.

Glen Tenove is now through playing football and is spending the majority of his time and effort playing a much more crucial game —the game of life. But do you know what? He's just as intense and competitive now as he was back in school, and he continues to strive for perfection. Life is a game in which production and not potential is rewarded, and that's Tenove's kind of game.

One final remark about Tenove — he is now pursuing a professional boxing career, and is undefeated, winning every fight by a knockout. Someday I guarantee he'll be the world champ, if he wants to be, for Glen Tenove demonstrates in a boxing ring what he demonstrates in life. He's not in there to prove his strength —he's in there to win the fight!

This brings us to the fourth and final answer to "Why can't I do it?" — "I didn't believe that I could really do it."

Believe in Yourself

Even if we know where we're going and what we want, and even if we want it badly enough, we'll never be able to do it if we don't believe we can. If you analyze each of the four answers to "Why can't I do it?" you'll realize they all have to do with the believing mind. The reason we can't do something is simply because our minds won't let our bodies do it. Remember, our actions start in our minds. In order for us to do it, we must remove all doubt and realize that the things we think about are the things we do, that we are what we think we are, and that we do only what we believe we can do. Napoleon Hill put it perfectly: "Whatever the mind of man can conceive and believe, the hand of man can achieve." This is true regardless if we receive positive or negative encouragement.

How many times in your life have you heard the words, "You can't do it," "You're wasting your time," or "Who are you fooling?" And how many times did you listen and believe it?

In a "Dear Abby" column was a list of famous people who at some point in their lives also heard the words, "You can't do it," "It's impossible. Why even try?" or "You're stupid and dumb." But it didn't matter, because they believed — and achieved!

Cripple him, and you have a Sir Walter Scott.

Lock him in a prison cell, and you have a John Bunyan.

Bury him in the snows of Valley Forge, and you have a George Washington.

Raise him in abject poverty, and you have an Abraham Lincoln.

Strike him down with infantile paralysis, and he becomes a Franklin D. Roosevelt, the only President of the U.S. to be elected to four terms.

When he is a lad of eight, burn him so severely in a school-house fire that the doctors say he will never walk again, and you have a Glen Cunningham, holder of the world's record in 1934 for running a mile in four minutes and six point seven seconds.

Deafen a genius composer, who continued to compose some of the world's most beautiful music, and you have a Ludwig Van Beethoven.

Drag him more dead than alive out of a rice paddy in Vietnam, and you have a Rocky Blyer, that awesome running back who just retired from the Pittsburgh Steelers.

Have him or her born black in a society filled with racial discrimination, and you have a Booker T. Washington, Harriet Tubman, Marian Anderson, George Washington Carver, or Martin Luther King, Jr.

Have him born of parents who survived a Nazi concentration camp, paralyze him from the waist down when he is four, and you have the incomparable concert violinst, Itzhak Perlman.

Call him a slow learner, retarded, and write him off as uneducable, and you have an Albert Einstein.

Some of the greatest men and women of our time have been saddled with disabilities and adversities but have managed to overcome them. It didn't matter what others thought or what labels were placed on them. They still were able to do it!

And why did they succeed? Because they had a positive mental attitude (PMA) and sincerely believed in themselves. PMA is the most important ingredient in all success, and as you hear more and more stories about successful people, you will realize that no one is, has been, or ever will be successful in their lives until they develop this attitude and firmly believe they can do it.

Attitude is a positive or negative feeling that causes a like action and a like result. We acquire these attitudes by doing or thinking the same thing over and over. For example, if we do something that produces success and continue to do it, it becomes a good habit and a positive attitude. The opposite action and result is also true. What we believe or what others make us believe about ourself is what determines our attitude and habitual response.

We Are What We Think We Are

I was part of a leadership seminar where we proved this to ourselves. The seminar moderator, Dave Mickel, carefully selected four participants from the group and arranged them in a circle in the middle of the room. He then took cardboard signs with strings and hung one around the neck of each participant. Each person in the circle could see the signs on the other three, but he was not to look at his own sign. The signs indicated personality traits that each was to have for a special task they were to do. The personality traits assigned to each person were different from that person's genuine personality.

The group was then given an assignment. In five minutes they were to plan a party, including agenda, location, and who would do what.

Regardless of the correct personality or talents of the individuals in the group, they were treated exactly as their labels said they should be treated. One label said, "Great leader; can take charge and organize." Another was labeled, "Great idea person; very intelligent, good mind and imagination." Another was labeled, "Never serious; irresponsible; talks too much." And the last sign labeled the participant, "Stupid; dumb; don't listen to me."

Do you know what happened? (Remember, the participants' personalities were totally different from their labels.) Within three minutes, because they were being treated a certain way, and because they were expected to be a certain way, they became frustrated with fighting back with their real personalities and started acting as their labels dictated. Every single one of them changed! The guy who was normally shy and a follower was given the leadership label and by the end of the exercise, he was a great leader. The girl who was normally very intelligent and outgoing was labeled "stupid." Surprisingly enough, she, too, conformed her actions to what others expected of her and seemed dumb!

It's true — we are what we think we are. We act like we think we should act. We become what we believe we can become. It's all up to us! It's all in our state of mind.

> If you think you are beaten, you are.
> If you think you dare not, you don't.
> If you like to win
> But think you can't
> It's almost a cinch you won't.
> If you think you'll lose, you have lost.
> For out in the world you'll find,
> Success begins with a person's will.
> It's all in the state of mind.
> Think big and your deeds will grow.
> Think small and you'll fall behind.
> Think that you can, and you will.
> It's all in the state of mind.
> If you think you're outclassed, you are.
> You've got to think big to rise.
> You've got to believe in yourself,
> Before you can win a prize.
> Life's battles don't always go
> To the stronger or fastest man.
> But sooner or later the man who wins
> Is the man who thinks he can.

There are three groups of people in the world. Some people will always exercise a proper positive mental attitude in their lives, and they are the successful giants of our age. Others will start and see PMA work for them for a short time, but one major setback eventually changes their attitude from positive to negative. They lose faith in themselves, fail to realize that success is maintained by those who keep using PMA, and quit. And finally, the vast majority of people everywhere have never really used PMA in their lives. They are not aware of this tremendous power found within themselves that can assure them success and happiness.

Dan's Own Story

I was one of these. Throughout my life I constantly heard from everyone, "You can do it. Just think positively, and you'll succeed, or "You can do it if you really want to," or "Your body will do what your mind tells it to do."

And do you know what? I didn't believe a word they were saying! I always thought they were just a bunch of rah-rah types — until one day a couple of years ago.

I was playing football at the University of Utah. I had been the starting defensive end as a sophomore, and was now entering my junior year. Things had been going well for me as an athlete, which excited me, because I wanted to play professional football more than anything else in the world. And if I had continued as I had been going, many felt I could have been drafted and had a successful career as a pro. I had heard from several of the pro teams and was working out hard, trying to make my dream come true.

It was April, the beginning of spring practice. I was the biggest I had ever been, 6'5", 245 pounds. I was the strongest I had ever been. I was bench-pressing 340 pounds, and I was one of the fastest men on the team. Things were really looking good for me, and I was excited about my future.

Halfway through the first day of practice we finally got to hit. We, the linebackers and defensive ends, divided up into two lines. I was at the head of one line, and the other starting end was at the head of the other. We were about twenty yards apart. The coach blew the whistle, and at full speed we collided head on and landed on the ground — just your basic tackling drill. Except that this time, the only parts of our bodies that made contact were his helmet and my right shoulder. As I lay there on the ground, I realized something was wrong — really wrong! My right arm was totally numb from my hand all the way up to my shoulder, neck, and even into my face. I couldn't feel anything and if that wasn't bad enough, my right eye drooped and I had loss of speech — I couldn't talk at all.

The trainer and coach came running over to me to see what was wrong, and when I looked up and saw four people instead of two, I really got worried. When one asked me what was wrong, I cleared my throat and told him, "Razzo flippo mardon reeka zulu pon." I couldn't talk very well! The trainer looked at me and asked again, "What did you say?" I told him again, "Flapakey soradol zongeezee maura." He laughed for a second and said, "You'd better come over here with me and sit down for a while."

As I was sitting there, still totally numb from my eye down to the end of my fingers, several players came over to see how I was. And when they asked, I told them, too: "Roof!" My speech sounded like a cross between Zambuchi and Pig Latin! I knew what I was trying to say, but what came out was totally foreign. What a joke!

I remained this way for almost half an hour, until finally my eye returned to normal and my speech came back. But my right arm and shoulder were still totally numb, and my arm dangled helplessly at my side. Deeply concerned, the trainer sent me over to the team doctor's office for my first examination and opinion. I say my first examination, because before I was through, I had visited sixteen of the top orthopedic sports medicine surgeons, neurologists, and physical therapists in the country, including the Los Angeles Rams' team doctors. All of the doctors had different theories but they did agree on one thing. I had severely injured the nerve that controls the shoulder muscle, and my arm would always be paralyzed. They also agreed on something else — there was no hope of rehabilitation. They expected no more than a 10 percent return of arm function and each said I definitely could not play football again. My arm and shoulder would always be like this and there was nothing I could do to rehabilitate it. They told me it was a freak injury and that I should face the facts. I should stop fooling myself with hope and accept the circumstances as they were. My arm would always be like this, I could never play football again, and there was nothing I could do to change it. I repeat myself here because that's all the doctors kept repeating to me.

As you can imagine, this broke my heart. I had played football three hours a day for thirteen years and now they said I was through. It was hard to accept but it soon started proving itself true.

During this month, my bench press fell from 340 pounds to where I couldn't even press the bar (it weighs forty-five pounds). My condition continued to get worse and my arm still hung by my side, limp and lifeless.

I continued to attend school, but I was always embarrassed because my arm just dangled as I walked to my classes. I put it in my pocket to stop the wiggling, but my elbow still moved and shook. Two months had now passed, and by this time my arm had atrophied to the point where it looked like a skinny noodle. In fact, my whole body started losing weight. I got so skinny I had to jump around in the shower to get wet!

One doctor had a special harness brace made for me which he called an airplane splint. It consisted of two big metal straps that hooked around my chest. These straps propped up a metal platform which held my arm straight out in front of me as if I was riding a bike. This experience of wearing the airplane splint was short-lived, though, because every time I walked past the library plaza on campus, one of the guys sitting there would start making sounds like a motorcycle — "Brrroom, brrroom . . ." To top it off, I went to my political science class that day, got to feeling restless, and leaned back in my chair. As I tilted back, my arm went up into the air. Thinking I wanted to ask a question, the teacher asked me, "Yes." Hey, that's all it took! I knew I'd had enough. I went home and took it off.

Several months went by and all I'd heard was, "No, no, no. Your shoulder and arm will always be like this. They will never get better." The sad and frustrating part was that I believed what the doctors were telling me. I think this was the major reason for my prolonged condition. My shoulder wasn't getting better because I didn't believe it could.

During this period, my injury was not only affecting my football, but it was also affecting the rest of my life. I couldn't think clearly or concentrate on doing any homework because it hurt so bad. I couldn't write because I was right-handed. Sure, it was a physical injury, but it was stopping me from doing anything else, and my attitude, enthusiasm, and dedication to life were quickly going downhill. I eventually hit rock bottom and felt like I didn't want to go on.

Because of my depression, friends were constantly trying to help me, and I appreciated their concern. But nothing worked until one friend let me listen to a tape he had by the great Zig Ziglar, the famous motivational teacher. As I listened, something started to happen. For the first time in many months I was excited and enthused. In fact, after hearing the tape, I was in tears. Ziglar had performed another miracle!

I know it's hard to believe, but that tape gave me renewed strength. As I related what Zig Ziglar said to my present predicament, I realized that doctors don't heal anyone, they just give us what we need to help us heal ourselves. The power comes from within us. All we have to do is figure out a way to get it out. Zig had given me new energy and hope for life.

Since that day my goal was to meet Zig Ziglar, and I have done that. In fact, we are now friends and have spent some time together. I love him dearly and highly recommend his book, *See You at the Top*, and materials to you. I think you'll understand why Mr. Ziglar means so much to me as I finish my story.

Almost miraculously, about this time I met another doctor, the seventeenth, who, in the opinion of many, is the finest orthopedic surgeon in the West. His name is Dr. Brent Pratley. He gave me new hope and a "nothing-to-lose" attitude to try to make my arm work as no other doctor had given me before. He told me my arm would get better if I worked at it, so I did.

With Zig's powerful words teamed up with Dr. Pratley's medical hope, what did I have to lose? Therefore, with this new determination, I went to my bedroom and began what would be a long but rewarding self-invented rehabilitation program. For the first time in over a year since the injury had occurred, I believed I could lift my arm. I believed I could do it, which was more than half the battle. Now all I had to do was do it!

I sat on my bed, concentrated as best I could, took a deep breath, and with all the strength I could muster, I struggled and shook to lift my arm as high as it would go. I lifted until I could lift no more. But instead of having to repeat that three-inch height again, I propped my arm up on a pillow while I rested, and then struggled to lift it higher.

As this process continued, the height of my arm got higher and higher until I had achieved my goal. It took me seven hours to get my arm above my head, but I did it! I was totally exhausted, but I think that was one of the happiest days of my life.

There I sat with pillows, books, clocks, and boxes stacked one on top of the other to serve as a support tower for my arm to rest on. I'm sure it was quite a sight!

The next day I followed the same process, and it took me only five hours to lift my arm above my head, so I was making progress and I was excited!

After about four weeks of this, I was able to swing my arm up above my head ten times in four or five minutes. After another two weeks, I was so proud and excited about what I could do that I went to a physical therapist to show him. He watched closely, examined my motions, and told me I was cheating. He said I couldn't do it, that it was impossible to do what I was doing unless I was rotating my arm and using my biceps muscle to lift it. You see, I still didn't have a shoulder muscle. It had atrophied because of the severe nerve damage. With no nerve, there is no muscle reaction, and with no muscle exercise, the muscle loses its size and strength. My right arm looked like it had two elbows. A bone stuck up where my shoulder muscle used to be.

Having the therapist tell me I was cheating really ticked me off! I'd worked so hard to do what I could do and now it wasn't good enough! What he told me wasn't bad, though, because it renewed my determination to prove him wrong, too!

Back to my room I went, and within two weeks I could lift my arm without rotating it. The weight room was the next test. Standing in front of the mirror to check my posture and arm motion, I began working up to ten repetitions with a two and one-half pound disc in each hand, in a butterfly flapping motion. When I could do it ten times, I moved up to a five-pound, then a ten-pound, and a fifteen-pound weight. Within a few months, I could raise my arm ten times above my head with twenty-pound dumbbells. How I did it no one knows. The doctors and therapists couldn't figure it out. My right arm now has complete feeling, with the exception of my shoulder area. It is still numb because the nerve is still severed. I have little if any shoulder muscle, but that doesn't matter. I have the complete use of my arm. Doctor Pratley recently checked me and declared a 97 percent return in rehabilitation.

I used to be a baseball pitcher. I wasn't able to throw a ball for three years, but now I can. In fact, I can even throw a curve. My bench press is up to 300 pounds again. How do I do it? How does my shoulder work? How can I move and work my arm without a nerve to contract the muscle? No one knows nor can they explain it. But I can and there's only one answer why. I can because *I believe I can.* I believe I can lift it. I believe I can throw a ball, arm wrestle, lift weights, bowl, shovel snow, and do anything else I want to do. And I also believe that the second I stop believing that I can do it, I won't be able to do it. I have programmed my brain just like I would a computer. When we believe something, our minds will do everything they can to prove it. This is what's happening in my body. My mind is telling my shoulder, "Listen, buddy, I don't care what you look like or what you don't have in there, you move that arm! There are no excuses, just move the arm and don't give me any flack!"

You see, it's all in my mind. It all has to do with having a proper positive mental attitude and with following the basic steps we've already talked about.

I first overcame my fear. Then I decided what I wanted and needed to do. I put myself in a specific direction (remember the alley or fairway?) to keep me on course to accomplish the task. I then committed that I wanted to do it badly enough. And finally, I firmly believed I could do it. I was willing to do anything, including going through pain and agony if necessary, to achieve what I believed.

And what was the result? I did it! This one experience changed my life. I was able to take a negative, devastating experience and turn it into a positive, valuable experience. I wasn't able to go on and play professional football as I had dreamed about, but I feel I received a much greater reward instead. I now have an unwavering proper positive mental attitude and know I can do anything in this world I want to if I think I can.

This is how I got involved traveling around the country speaking to people about the steps to success. Remember, I used to be the guy who didn't believe all that rah-rah cheerleading "you-can-do-it" stuff. But now I know it works. I've proven it to myself, and now I'm teaching others.

In fact, the combination of positive thinking and the following of the steps outlined in this chapter is the secret to successful living and the guarantee that the next time someone leans over and says to you, "You can do it," you will be able to do just that — do it! Remember, you were born to succeed and succeed and succeed!

Chapter Seven

"Who Am I?"

How to Develop a Good Self-Concept

Have you noticed lately that no matter where you go, you can't do anything in total quiet? You go to the store to buy food, and music is playing there. You go to another store to buy clothes, and different music is playing. You make a phone call, they put you on hold, and what do you hear? Music. Doctors' and dentists' offices play music. And now even elevators play the top forty tunes. Why? It is only because they want to be courteous? No way! People in our society are afraid to be alone with themselves. When it's dead quiet, they are forced into being alone with themselves and they don't like this for fear they won't like who they are.

Psychologists tell us that most people never take the time and trouble to figure out who they are and what they want out of life. In fact, some people give more time to selecting a TV program than to doing their schoolwork, planning their careers, working on their talents, or discovering themselves and becoming the best they can be. But if we are ever to get the very most out of life, we must know who we are and form an opinion about ourselves.

Changing Your Self-Concept

The May 1975 *Readers Digest* carried this statement: "A twenty-five-year hard-line study at Harvard University, under the guidance of David McMilland, established precise scientific verification that you can change motivation by changing the way you think about yourself."

How we feel about ourselves is what we refer to as self-concept, and understanding self-concept is the answer to "Who am I?"

Because knowing who you are is crucial to your success and happiness, this comprehensive chapter covers most areas of how to answer this question. But before we begin, you've got to loosen up and learn not to take yourself so seriously.

I was very tall and thin in high school and played running back on the football team. During one game I was being annoyed by the constant attention of a small dog. He followed me everywhere.

At last, when play had moved to the other end of the field, I turned and shouted to the spectators, "Whoever owns this dog, will you please call him off."

To this, a voice responded, "Come here, Spot. Them ain't bones, boy, them's legs."

Another such experience of not taking ourselves too seriously is a pro celebrity golf tournament that my friend Jeff attempted to play in. I say "attempted" because Jeff was an All-American football player in college and a third-round draft choice by the NFL St. Louis Cardinals, but he couldn't quite catch the vision of golf. As he puts it, "Hitting a little white ball as far as you can so you can chase it just isn't my idea of a good time." But because he was a good sport, Jeff went ahead and played in the tourney.

On the first tee, there were about 400 people assembled to watch the golfers begin the course. Finally it was Jeff's turn. He stepped out onto the grass, put his ball on the tee, took a mighty swing, and "whiffed." That's right, he missed the ball! He then concentrated harder and took another mighty swing, only to "whiff" again. With even more determination, he shuffled his feet, took a third giant swing — but yes, he missed again, this time blowing the ball off the tee. As Jeff stooped over to put the ball back onto the tee, he made everyone laugh when he looked up at the crowd and said, "Tough course, isn't it?"

Finally he hit the ball (it flew off the edge of his club and almost hit a lady) and proceeded to play. During the walk toward the second green there was another humorous conversation between Jeff and his caddy. Jeff: "Terrible course, caddy, terrible." His caddy's reply as they walked through the rough: "Well, sir, not really. You haven't been on it for over an hour."

The final episode of this amusing story came at the conclusion of the third hole where Jeff got a 12 on a par 3. After hitting his ball into the trap and playing in the sand for a few minutes, he asked what time it was. And when his caddy said three o'clock, Jeff decided to call quits. He had teed off on the first hole at twelve noon and was already on his sixth ball — he had lost all the others. Therefore, he dropped his clubs, sat down, laughed at himself and joked with the spectators for a while, stood up, walked to the parking lot, paid the caddy, and drove home.

You see, part of "Who am I?" is human. It must be accepted and sometimes laughed at, as it sometimes makes funny human mistakes. So don't take yourself too seriously. Keep this in mind as you begin to discover yourself.

To better understand what is meant by self-concept, let's define each of the two words. First, *self*. According to the dictionary, *self* means "One's self; (me, myself, and I). The essential person, distinct from all other persons in identity."

The second word of this phrase, *concept*, means a thought or an idea. When put together, we find *self-concept* to mean what your opinion is of you.

You may be wondering why I would take time to discuss self-concept when there are so many other topics to cover. The reason is that the majority of people who walk the halls of life, probably nine out of ten, have a poor self-concept. By this I mean that they see themselves, either through action or words, as not being as good as others. Whether they developed this complex while they were growing up through peer pressure and lack of group acceptance, or whether it came through their interaction with parents and brothers and sisters, somehow, some way, they gained that feeling of inferiority.

Why is it that so many young people have a poor self-concept? I've pondered this for years. You see, I've had stretches in my life when my self-concept was not what it should be; when I didn't really like myself as I should. There have been times when I have had problems with the questions, What do I represent? and Who do I want to be? And times when my self-worth, self-esteem, and self-acceptance faltered and failed. But why? What caused this feeling of inferiority to come over me and almost ruin my life? The answer for me is the answer for everyone.

People who have a poor self-concept have these feelings because they do not realize the awesome potential that rests within them. They don't understand the definition for the word *self:* "Self is distinct from all other persons in identity." In other words, you are unique and special, and this makes you important.

If it were possible for you to travel throughout this world and shake the hand of every person who is alive today, you would never meet another you. In fact, if you could meet everyone who has ever lived, estimated at sixty-eight billion people, or meet everyone who is yet to live on the earth, you still would never meet another you. There has never been a duplication of an individual since man began. Think about how important that makes you. When you are gone, no one can replace you. Life is like a giant jigsaw puzzle and every person on earth is one piece of it. No one else can ever fill your unique slot.

Our Own Private World

We also need to understand that each of us lives in a world that is like no other world. We're with ourselves twenty-four hours a day, and each day we have the say-so in what we do. That makes us the creators of our own little world that has never been in existence before. Did you know the average person can speak between two hundred and four hundred words per minute, and think about two thousand words per minute? So even when you are doing something or talking with someone, no one else ever really knows all that you're thinking and all that you want to do and say. They only see and hear a small portion of your

thoughts. Therefore, the only person who knows everything about you is you. You have complete control over that
inner world. This makes you the master of your own
destiny because you have the freedom to create any kind of
world you please. For example, far too many people are the
creators of garbage worlds. That's all they have because
that's what they've created, and they have no one else to
blame but themselves. They have allowed and sometimes
welcomed garbage to be dumped into their heads.

This includes garbage like vulgar words; filthy "blue"
jokes, songs and stories; unkind and untrue tales about
their neighbors; "foldout" pictures; and "sick" comments
about the opposite sex.

What happens when you have a head full of garbage
words and junk stories? Simply, if garbage goes in, it's a
sure bet it has to come out. You'll speak garbage, think
garbage, drink garbage, and associate in low-budget
garbage places with garbage-head friends.

>With garbage and junk
>Our big can is well fed
>This trash we don't want
>We can burn it instead
>But what about dirt
>That you've heard or you've said
>Oh, what can be done
>With a garbage-can head?

If you're one of these garbage heads, don't take offense
at what I say. I used to be one, too. Just change — pull your
head out! It's never too late to change your ways and
become the best you can be. If you need assistance, just
remember the already-mentioned statement: "No matter
what your past has been, you have a spotless future." That's
important to know! If you don't like who you are and what
you're becoming; if you don't like what you've done or the
world you've created for yourself; if you feel your past is
ugly and degrading; forget about it! Remember, everyone
has a past. If you look back, soon you'll be going that way. It
cannot be changed. Therefore, look ahead to your spotless
future and concentrate on what you now choose to do and
be. As you do, you will see that you can change your attitude,
which changes your self-concept, which changes your whole
life.

Understand and Change Yourself

How does this come about? It comes with understanding your own worth and realizing that when you make a mistake, you should not childishly blame yourself. You should not downgrade the product (you), merely because you haven't used it (your life) properly. You don't discard and throw away a piano or a guitar just because two of its strings are out of key. Instead, you take time to tune it up now, and only look ahead to the beautiful music that will flow from it. Remember, there is a difference between the person and the performance.

Another crucial part of your self-concept development goes beyond how you see yourself. It involves what others think of you and how you are perceived by others. Whether you believe it or not, what people say to you or about you can make or break you. If you don't believe them, they can't hurt you. This statement is true: "Sticks and stones may break my bones but names will never hurt me." However, if you do believe what others tell you, their words can and will hurt you if you let them. Here's an example just to show you what can happen: Today you're sitting in my office, and the phone rings. On the other end of the line is a police officer with some news about the person in your life who is nearest and dearest to you. The officer tells me that this person has just been brutally murdered, and he asks me if I will pass this on to you.

What would be your reaction to this story if I were to present you with the news and you didn't believe me? If you didn't believe me, and didn't let the news into your mind, you probably would be sitting there smiling and joking around. It would have no effect on you. No matter how serious I was when I told you, and no matter how shocking I made it sound, if you didn't let it in your mind, it would not and could not hurt you.

On the other hand, what is the most serious thing that could happen to you in hearing such news, letting it in your mind, and believing it? You could have a heart attack, a stroke, or something else. You could even go into shock and die. It's true! The effect of the news could be so drastically terrible that it could shock you literally to death.

So here we have the two sides of the story. On one side I

112

have you laughing and joking around. You're not affected in any way by the news. You don't believe it, and you never let it in your mind. But on the other hand, I have you lying on the floor, dead.

I ask, What did I do to you? The answer is — nothing! All I did was pass on words. In one instance you were not affected by my words, and in the other instance, you were killed by them. Why? How can the same exact words in the same exact circumstances have two completely different outcomes?

The answer is because in one instance you kept the words and thoughts out of your mind, and in the other instance you let them in and believed them.

What does this tell us about our words and thoughts? How powerful are they? Words and thoughts rule the world! In fact, the world is made up of nothing more than words and thoughts. Therefore, be cautious with what you say and believe and remember this power as you start to develop your self-concept. For if you do, you'll be able to screen, sift, and weigh what others say to you, which gives you total control of yourself.

Because you have complete control of your mind, no one can make you feel inferior without your own consent. No one else can get you to see yourself in any other way other than *your* way. This means if you don't like who you are, you can change by simply changing your self-concept. Start telling yourself that you're great, that you can do it, that you are going to change, that you're going to be this new way. And if you do it long enough, your brain will take these signals and statements as facts and start doing everything it can to prove them true. This is how our brains run our bodies. For example, we don't feel with our fingers or smell with our noses. We don't hear with our ears, nor do we see with our eyes. And for you women who are constantly on diets trying to lose weight, your appetite is not in your stomach. All of this happens in the brain. Our limbs and other parts of our bodies act only as transmitters and receptors. This is why you can change your actions and self-concept by changing what goes into your brain. Its powers are incalculable! Because the brain is so amazing and powerful, let's continue the discussion about it that we began in Chapter 5. The more we know about the brain and how it works, the better we'll be able to use it for our good.

Hypnotism and Life Style Changes

As you recall, the average human brain has unlimited potential. To help us understand this potential and the importance that positive thinking and input play in helping us reach it, let's look at what hypnotism teaches us. Any of you who have seen a hypnotist at work will surely agree they are amazing and seemingly magic. But realistically, hypnotism is nothing more than someone getting another person to completely, and without reservation, believe in their words as total truth. Through trust and concentration, the hypnotist suggests to the mind of the hypnotized, and they respond by doing whatever they're asked to do.

The three examples below were used in each of the three hypnotist shows I've seen, and each proves that a person can and will do whatever he thinks and believes he can do.

The hypnotist tells a shy, timid introvert that she is an exceptional orator, a great entertainer, and a humorist. What is the result? This quiet, intimidated soul (attested to by her friends in the audience) is suddenly transformed into an extroverted speaker who is now hard to shut up! She says more in the next five minutes than she's said all year!

An obvious question, then, is did the hypnotist add anything to the girl's potential? Did he, in five seconds, miraculously teach her how to speak and tell jokes? No! All the hypnotist did was help the girl overcome the negative idea and negative self-belief that she couldn't do what she just did. How did he do it? Simply by suggesting a positive thought to the girl's mind that she believed as truth. This positive thought replaced the negative, and she responded accordingly.

Another friend of mine who has a tough time adding simple math problems with pencil and paper is hypnotized. Suddenly, he adds, multiplies, and divides three-digit numbers with incredible speed and accuracy, all in his head. He becomes a math whiz in a matter of seconds. How? Does the hypnotist give him a crash course in mathematics? No! The hypnotist simply tells him he can do it, breaks down the self-constructed barrier that's been holding him back, and lets him use his previously suppressed potential.

The last demonstration is with two strong football buddies who are made weak by the hypnotist's suggestion to their minds that they are weak. Normally they can lift hundreds of pounds, but now, because of a negative thought placed in their minds, they can't even lift a rubber ball or a three-ounce shoe off the table.

The mind controls our muscles and when the brain says they can't do something, they really can't do it. In this instance the muscles that are used to lift the ball or shoe are out of order because the brain says they are. They actually contract to the point where there is no available movement or strength. In reverse, new strength to the weakling comes the same way.

What can we conclude about the mind from these true-life, documented hypnotic demonstrations? Simply, we can do anything we make up our minds to do. We have the potential to do the impossible if we firmly believe and positively know that we can. Remember, the hypnotist didn't do anything to make the persons he hypnotized change in strength, knowledge, or experience. All he did was suggest a positive or negative thought to their minds.

Each of us is also hypnotized in a very real sense. Just as if we were under a hypnotic spell, we do only what we tell ourselves we can do. Therefore, if you're negative, introverted, uncoordinated, weak, stupid, or slow, it's because you choose to be. And because it's up to you, *you can change!*

If you're presently self-hypnotized to fail and be negative; if you feel unsure, intimidated, and not "up to par," just rehypnotize yourself to be exactly the way you want to be. Suggest some new and positive images to your mind. It only takes a hypnotist a few seconds to perform miracles of change, and therefore, if you want to change badly enough and truly believe you can, it shouldn't take you much longer. Within you right now lies the potential to succeed and do whatever your dreams tell you you can do.

Now that you comprehend the enormous powerful capacity the brain possesses, let's examine the way it works.

The brain has three main parts that perform three distinct functions.

Conscious Mind

All information that comes in from the five senses and enters the brain is immediately analyzed by the conscious mind. As the information comes in, the conscious mind dips into the subconscious mind to see what else is stored in there that relates to what you are now seeing, touching, smelling, tasting, or hearing.

Subconscious Mind

Everything you've ever seen, touched, smelled, tasted, or heard from the time you were two years old is stored in the subconscious mind. It's reality as you've seen it in the past. It receives information from the conscious mind, judges it, evaluates it, and arrives at a conclusion of what reality is *now*. The most important thing to remember about the subconscious is that it does not differentiate between a real experience and an imagined one. Everything is real and accepted as fact.

Creative Subconscious Mind

Its function is to oversee the interaction between the conscious and the subconscious minds. It makes sure that your actions (coming from the conscious) agree with reality as you have perceived it (coming from the subconscious). The creative role it plays is making sure the incoming data agree with reality by changing the "slant" or perception of the incoming data, if needs be, to carry on its duties. The creative subconscious keeps a person appearing to be sane. For when a person acts different than he thinks, people call him inconsistent and insecure. The creative subconscious mind keeps the actions agreeing with the thoughts. Because of the creative subconscious mind, many people only hear and see what they want to.

For example, a mother with a new baby goes to sleep at night. Her house is next to a freeway where large buses, trucks, and loud automobiles continuously rumble by. Even low-flying jets on their way to the nearby airport shake the house as they soar past. Yet the mother sleeps soundly. However, the second her new baby makes the slightest sound, she immediately awakens and gets up to check on the child. She hears only what she wants to hear.

Let's put this knowledge into practice and begin to use our brain power to improve our self-concept. How do you change your unwanted behavior to something else? How do you change yourself from an unsuccessful person into a successful person?

Input and Output Are the Same

It all boils down to what goes into your brain. Our brains are computers, and computers do only what they are programmed to do. No matter how big a computer is, it can only do what the computer programmer tells it to do. Input always equals output — what goes in must eventually come out!

If your input is "I can't, I'm unsuccessful, I'm fat, I'm stupid," the output will be the same. When you put a negative thought into your brain, the subconscious mind does everything it can to prove it to be real. Then, the creative subconscious mind makes sure your actions, which in this case are negative, agree with reality. The result is that you act like a loser, you are unsuccessful, you say stupid things, and you act immature. That's how you perceive yourself — that's how you are. And it's all because of your input.

Now let's reverse it. Your input is "I can, I'm successful, I'm trim, I'm smart and intelligent." The subconscious takes it as fact and does everything it can to prove that you're actually what you think you are. Then the creative subconscious makes sure your actions agree with your thoughts. The result: you *are* smart and intelligent, you *are* successful, you *are* the person you perceive yourself to be. And again, it's all because of your input.

If you want to change, just program your subconscious mind to perceive yourself the way you want to be. Remember, it doesn't know the difference between real and imagined. To your subconscious mind, everything is always real! Think about the way you want to be, concentrate on it, and constantly feed it into your subconscious mind. If you do it for twenty-one to thirty days, you will change and be the way you want to be. Let's look at a realistic example.

If you want to lose weight, you don't have to go on one of the fad diets. Remember that your appetite and craving for

117

food is not in the stomach, it is in the brain. So program your mind to see yourself at a certain weight, concentrate on that weight every day (especially at meal time), and let your brain do the rest. It doesn't care that you really weigh 150. If you can imagine and tell yourself that you only weigh 115, your subconscious mind believes you; it takes everything as fact and does not differentiate between imagined and real. And when the new programmed input weight is 115 pounds, it discards the old input, automatically changes, and starts doing everything to prove the new input true. Because the brain controls the appetite, your appetite will now decrease to satisfy only 115 pounds of calories instead of 150 pounds. The creative subconscious mind then finishes the task by making sure your actions agree with your thoughts, resulting in your watching what and how much you eat. You're not as hungry anymore and don't need to consume as much to get full, and you're well on your way to attaining your "dream" weight. The only thing remaining in this natural diet program is exercise.

If you want to change in a hurry and speed up this reprogramming process, write out a "positive affirmation" — a statement on paper suggesting to your brain exactly the goal in mind. For example: "I am beautiful and skinny. I only weigh 115 pounds." Read it several times a day; keep it visible and always in your thoughts. Soon it will become reality to your subconscious mind and the rest will be easy. You'll become that kind of person, change your self-concept, and be who you want to be. As was already mentioned, it takes approximately twenty-one to thirty days to reprogram your mind. Therefore, start now and test it out. I guarantee this works! And it works not only in weight loss, but also in every endeavor in life.

You can accomplish anything if you just learn to use and control your mind. All you have to do is want to change. And when you decide that, it's simple to do so. You only need to follow three steps.

Do It — Now — Don't Fear Change

The first step is to *do it!* It's simple, but for some reason, few people ever do. They are always in the planning stage and never in the go stage. They just talk and wish and never get anything done. Don't be like this — change that trend and put your plans into action now, even if you're still planning. You'll find that all your plans will fall into place tomorrow if you're actively accomplishing what you need to do today.

This brings us to the second step. *Do it now!* Why procrastinate? If you're going to change, why not get started right away?

The author Oliver Wendell Holmes felt that the majority of mankind do not become the best they can be. He said, "The great tragedy of life is that the average person goes to his grave with the music still in him." In other words, every person has an oil reserve of talent inside him, but most people never drill a well to let the oil come out. They never uncork the bottle. They just continue doing the same old thing, time after time, day after day, year after year.

A few years ago I saw a sign I had heard much about. It was on a roadside near Jackson Hole, Wyoming, at a point where the paved road ended and a dusty, washed-out, winding dirt road began. The sign read, "Choose your rut now; you'll be in it for the next twenty miles." This really made me think. How many times in our lives do we let ourselves get into a rut? And as time passes, we become more and more content with our situation. We become too lazy or uncaring to change, and the rut just gets deeper and deeper.

I'm sure this has happened to everyone. And as I recall what happened to me, it's easy to realize that at the particular time in my life when I knew I should change, it was hard for me — at least I felt it was hard. I feared change; I was afraid of the unknown, and as a result I didn't change.

This brings us to the third and final step. If you fear change, then look at it differently and call it a different name. You see, changing is only psychological. It comes when a person decides that it's time to change. Change is not something that we should fear but something that we should welcome. *Change is nothing more than self-improvement.* We constantly need to evaluate ourselves, our situations, our desires, and our friendships. We need to see if we are still aimed in the correct direction to achieve our goals. If we are not, we must be willing to better ourselves and correct ourselves in every way we can.

In reaching out for this excellence, don't be afraid to let go of something if it's holding you back from accomplishing your goals. It may be a physical item, a habit, a moral code, or a philosophy. It may even be a friend. It's been said, "Some people think it's holding on that makes one stong. Sometimes it's letting go."

My friend Charlie tells a personal story about John, his idol in high school. John was a handsome, popular student athlete whom Charlie wanted to emulate.

One night Charlie was supposed to meet John at a party, but when he got there, John was nowhere to be found. When Charlie saw an ambulance drive up to the back of the house where the party was, he fought his way through the crowd to find out what the problem was all about. To his concern, there writhing on the floor was John, screaming out of control. The ambulance took John away, and Charlie asked what had happened.

John had a track scholarship to a major university in California and was an outstanding, clean-cut, all-American boy who never messed around with drugs. But this night, John's friends (who were also Charlie's friends) offered John some "angel dust" or PCP, one of the most deadly drugs going around the country. John at first said no, but after continual peer pressure and harassment from his "friends," he finally gave in to being called "chicken" and "sissy" and smoked it.

Sure, John had a few laughs for a minute, but he traded his whole life for them. From this one incident he suffered severe brain damage. He lost his scholarship, doesn't recognize his family, and his so-called friends can't help him now.

What is the point of this sad experience? As a result of it, Charlie did some soul-searching and decided that even though he loved these "friends" that were now into drugs, he must let them go, change his course, and find others to associate with. From this experience Charlie gave up a lot of things — a moral code and philosophy, a habit and health code, and many friends. But he did it because he knew he wanted to continually improve himself and become not what others wanted him to be, but who *he* wanted to be! Charlie didn't suddenly feel that he was too good for his old friends. He simply wanted more out of life and he had the courage to do what he had to do to get it.

Something else that will help you improve yourself is for you to constantly ask yourself, "Is this my best? Can I do better than I'm doing now or is this my very best possible effort?" If it's not your best, it should be easy to change, because you want to be the best you can be.

As I look back on my junior high and high school days, I remember them as a time of competing and comparing. Guys competed against guys, and girls compared themselves against girls. Everyone was competing in everything — clothes, boyfriends and girlfriends, gossip, grades, sports, and talents. Don't get me wrong. I realize the value of good head-to-head competition and how it helps us to become better people. We live in a competitive society, and we need to learn how to compete to survive.

Compete Against Yourself

However, the competition I experienced in the areas I listed above is shaky and doesn't necessarily contribute to a satisfying and productive life style until you first learn to compete against yourself. Concentrate now on competing against yourself. Don't compare yourself with others. You have personality and character traits that no one else has, so how can you ever begin to compare yourself with anyone other than yourself? It's not fair. It's like comparing fruit and machinery. They're totally different. The result you're seeking, remember, is to find out who *you* are and what *you* can do, and then to become the very best *you* can possibly be. When you compare yourself with others, regardless if you're extra smart or average, nothing but stifling, non-productive results can come of it.

A young man whose name will remain anonymous attended Olympus High School in Salt Lake City, Utah. He had an I.Q. of 167 — a genius. He breezed through high school easily with straight As and did it without much effort, never taking a book home. Everyone thought he was brilliant. Everyone looked up to him as far as an academic achiever and thought he was the "cat's meow."

But I ask you, was he? Was he really successful? If we are competing against others and manage to consistently beat them, is this what makes us the best?

This young man always got the highest scores on tests. In fact, in competition against others, he was always a standout. But that's not the important form of competition. That's not what inspires us to become the best we can be. You see, the straight As he was getting didn't point out that his high score on the test was only 75 out of 100. It didn't indicate that he missed twenty-five questions. It didn't represent the fact that this genius could have achieved a score of 100 out of 100 with a little bit of effort. What a waste! If only he could have understood the true form of competition — competition against himself. We shouldn't just run fast enough to win the race or just work hard enough to get the highest score. We should try to set a "personal best" — a world record each time we set foot on the racetrack of life.

Who Am I?

Discovering yourself and finding out who you are is a key in forming a good self-concept. Therefore, start by asking yourself the two questions we previously mentioned, but this time answer them as well. Ask yourself, "Who am I?" not "Who do my friends think I am?" or "Who do my parents and relative think I am?" but "Who do *I* know I am?" The second question is, "What do I represent?" not "What do I represent around my friends?" or "What are my values and moral codes and habits around my parents and family?" I want you to answer, "What do I stand for? What are my views? Am I consistent or am I trying to please everyone? Am I honest or am I a hyprocrite trying to fool everybody into thinking that I'm someone that I'm not? Am I wild around wild people, and straight around straight people?" Don't be a chameleon, always changing colors in different circumstances. You've got to be consistent and stable. You've got to be able to look yourself in the eye and like what you see.

> When you get what you want in your struggle for self
> And the world makes you King for a Day,
> Just go to the mirror and look at yourself,
> And see what the man has to say.

122

For it isn't your father or mother or wife
Whose judgment upon you must pass.
The fellow whose verdict counts most in your life
Is the one staring back from the glass.
You may be like Jack Horner and chisel a plum,
And think you're a wonderful guy,
But the man in the glass says you're only a bum,
If you can't look him straight in the eye.
He's the fellow to please, never mind all the rest,
For he's with you clear to the end.
And you've passed your most dangerous, difficult test
If the man in the glass is your friend.
You may fool the whole world down the pathway of years
And get pats on the back as you pass.
But your final reward will be heartaches and tears
If you've cheated the man in the glass.

Author Unknown

One key I've found that helps in discovering yourself is to remember your uniqueness we've talked so much about. You are important and special and you don't have to look elsewhere for happiness and satisfaction. By just being yourself, you can achieve all the happiness you want.

The late Emmett Kelly, who achieved worldwide fame as a sad-faced hobo clown called "Weary Willie," gave some great advice on being yourself. When all the other circus clowns looked basically alike, Kelly had a different idea — an idea he knew was right for him.
He explained:

What's the hardest thing in the world to be? I can tell you in one word, 'yourself,' especially if what you are is different from the crowd. But I'll guarantee this. If you can find the courage to be yourself, to be the person God intended you to be, you're going to come out all right. So if you ever worry about being different from the crowd, stop worrying! "Weary Willie" had almost a half century of fun just being himself, and so have I.

If you want to make life simple and easy for yourself, just discover you.

Be the Best of Whatever You Are

If you can't be a pine on the top of the hill,
Be a scrub in the valley — but be
The best little scrub by the side of the rill;
Be a bush if you can't be a tree.

If you can't be a bush be a bit of the grass,
And some highway happier make;
If you can't be a muskie then just be a bass —
But the liveliest bass in the lake!

We can't all be captains, we've got to be crew.
There's something for all of us here,
There's big work to do, and there's lesser to do,
And the task you must do is near.

If you can't be a highway then just be a trail,
If you can't be the sun be a star;
It isn't by size that you win or you fail —
Be the best of whatever you are!

                                        Author Unknown

Becoming the "best of whatever you are" is the most important part of developing a good self-concept, and it doesn't come easy. Those who have reached this point in life have done so through hard work, extra effort, and unwavering endurance.

For example, a young girl from Romania won five medals as a gymnast in the 1976 Olympic Games; three gold medals, one silver medal, and one bronze medal. Her name was Nadia Comaneci. But this is not the amazing part of Nadia's story. The amazing part is that she received seven perfect scores — a perfect ten points out of ten points possible. It was the first time in Olympic history that any gymnast had ever received a perfect score, let alone the seven that Nadia received. Think about this. She was only fifteen years old, and she was the greatest gymnast in the world!

Now I have a question. Was Nadia Comaneci always perfect? Could she always get a perfect score or do you think she had to work for it? How many times do you think she fell before she mastered her amazing and difficult routine? Let me answer this with another story.

In 1980 the University of Utah women's gymnastics team won the national championship and because of my continued involvement at the "U," I had several opportunities to watch the team work out.

One particular day, I'd been there a few minutes when I noticed a girl working on a certain exotic acrobatic move on the uneven parallel bars.

The move consisted of her swinging around on the upper bar twice to gain momentum, letting go of the bar, spreading her legs in a Chinese split position to avoid the lower bar, grabbing the lower bar as she flew through the air, swinging around the lower bar, letting go again, and finally grabbing the upper bar again to continue with her routine.

I'm telling you, it was some move to learn, and she was having an awful time figuring out how to do it! I watched her for over an hour as she tried time and time again to master it.

I watched as she climbed up on the bar, started twirling around, let go, spread her legs, reached up to grab the lower bar, and missed. She flew right past it and crashed! Her coach ran over, helped her up, encouraged her to try it again, and helped her climb back up on the bars. Again she began twirling to pick up speed, let go of the upper bar, spread her legs, flew through the air, grabbed for the lower bar, missed it, and crashed to the floor again. After about ten crashes, this girl was sobbing with pain and limping around. But this didn't stop her — I counted twenty-three times that it took her to learn this particular move. She had twenty-two brutal crashes before she finally did it right.

Can you imagine the pain she must have felt? And this was just to learn one of the many moves in her total routine! What about all the crashes I hadn't seen that she must have had as she tried to learn the other moves?

Well, to end this story, her efforts paid off — this girl went on to win a medal on the uneven parallel bars in the national championships. Her practice, hard work, and determination paid off.

The answer, then, to the question, Was Nadia Comaneci always perfect? is the same answer to the question, Was the U. of U. gymnast always the best in the nation? Of course not! Both girls had to work countless hours, persevere, and endure pain, hurt, and agony until they had pushed themselves to the limit. From a very young age until then, every hour of life had been spent striving to become the best they could possibly be.

Develop a Good Self-Concept

As we've discussed "Who am I?" in this chapter, I'm sure you'll agree that having a good self-concept is the key to successful living. If we feel good about ourselves, it's easy for us to feel good toward others. People with good, positive self-concepts are easy to spot. Their works and actions are readily recognizable. They have a mystical charisma, a magnetism that draws people to them. They are friendly, warm, and considerate. They know who they are and what they can do, and therefore, they don't spend time trying to prove it to anybody else.

People who have a good and stable self-concept understand the power of a smile, and they use it. They know a smile is language that everyone, from babies to great-grandparents, understand. They take great pride in how they look, how they act, what they say, and how they feel. They are careful, genuine, and honest in their dealings with their fellowmen, and they understand that you never get a second chance to make a first impression. They realize that people can see right through fraud, insincerity, and phony showmanship.

If this is how you want to be, start now by never telling yourself you can't do something. Never tell yourself that you're stuck and can't move. You can do anything you think you can. Where there's a will there's a way. And there's *always* a way. All you have to do is find it. I learned this from a very dear friend of mine. His name is Jan Smith.

Jan is an individual who was stuck in every sense of the word but who refused to stay that way. He overcame his enormous problems, found the way that he knew was there, and refused to settle for mediocrity. He knew the importance of discovering himself and having a good self-concept and then did everything he knew how to do to cultivate and maintain it. Even when he wanted to quit, because he knew who he was, he was able to hang in there and succeed.

Jan Smith is one of the greatest men I know. He was a great athlete in high school and again in college, where he accepted a football scholarship to play running back for BYU. When his eligibility was up, and because of his strong desire to help and teach young men, he dedicated

126

himself to becoming a football coach. In 1973, immediately after he graduated from college, he landed the football head coaching job at Morgan High School in the town of Morgan, Utah. All was going well for him. Jan had married a beautiful woman. They were settling in fine to the new job and location, and nothing could be better.

His first football game as a head coach was in the first week of September. As Jan diligently prepared himself and his team for that game, something started happening to his eyesight. He said it was like looking out a window that was foggy and covered with water spots. It lasted for quite some time, so he went to the doctor for an examination and waited two weeks for the diagnosis. On the day of his first game, the diagnosis came. The doctor told him he had either a brain tumor or multiple sclerosis. Two weeks later the final diagnosis was made — he had the incurable, dreaded disease, multiple sclerosis or MS.

MS is a disease that attacks virtually every muscle in the body. It starts in one area (in Jan's case, his eyes) and moves throughout the body until it totally consumes. Sometimes MS spreads fast and other times it moves slowly. In Jan's case it is still moving relatively slowly.

During the first year that his eyesight went bad, he was walking along and his leg gave way. He fell to the ground, got back up, and continued on his way. As time passed, this occurred more and more frequently until finally after two years, he could walk no more. But this didn't stop him. He purchased a golf cart to drive to school and around town; this also allowed him to continue his coaching. To this day he drives it right out onto the field and parks it on the sidelines.

Back in 1972, in his first year of coaching, Jan took his Morgan Trojans to the state finals, where he took second place, losing only to a much more powerful and experienced team. The next year came, and Jan once again started preparing for the season, only to be hindered as his eyesight and body grew weaker and weaker. Consequently, as most of us would, he became very discouraged. His condition was almost too much to bear, and he told his wife he was going to quit coaching and teaching and find something else to do.

This decision lasted awhile and stopped his progress in stabilizing the disease. As his reasons for living dwindled and his goals for the future became fewer, his life, health, and football team also suffered and took a turn for the worse. He lost football games and even fell back some in the game of life.

Finally, after a great deal of encouragement from his beautiful and supportive wife, his friends, and his ballplayers, Jan started to change his mind about quitting. Then came a letter in the mail from the national president of the Multiple Sclerosis Society which made his decision final. The letter was written by Ara Paraseghian, then the head football coach at Notre Dame. It was a short letter, but it said so much that it literally changed Jan's life. Coach Paraseghian said that "you don't coach with your body, you coach with your mind. And as long as you can think, you can be a great coach. Hang in there! You can do it!"

Because of this letter and the other "don't give up" influences in his life, Jan changed his outlook on his disease and decided that he was going to be a great football coach no matter what it took or how much it took out of him. He was going to be the best he could be!

This determination seemed to give him new energy and new excitement for life, and it rubbed off on his team. From 1973 to 1980, Jan's win/loss record was 74 wins and 26 losses. Since his first year at Morgan, he has made it into the state playoffs most years. He took second place in 1972 and again in 1976. The next year, in 1977, he finally won the whole thing, taking home the state championship trophy. In 1978 he made it again to the finals, but came short, taking second. And again, in 1980, he took second. But what happend in 1979? To put it lightly, Jan Smith and his Morgan Trojans were awesome! This was the year Jan demonstrated what he was really made of. With a somewhat average team, Jan Smith and "his boys" beat everybody that stood in their way. He took his team to an undefeated, untied, perfect season record of 12 wins and no losses, and easily won the Utah State High School Football Championship. This same year, Jan's incredible story was told and featured on well-known TV programs such as

"Real People," "Games People Play," and "That's Incredible!" NFL films did a special on this great man and his undying determination to be the best he could be. And as a fitting climax and tribute to Jan Smith, he was voted the 1981 Multiple Sclerosis Father of the Year and was flown back to Washington, D.C., to receive the honor from President Reagan himself. He truly is an inspiration to us all; he's a living, fighting testimony of the fact that you need to discover yourself, decide what you want to do, and then do it. Jan Smith proves the importance of living for a cause, and he demonstrates how much success a person can have in life regardless of obstacles and setbacks.

Use Your Knowledge

To tie a bow around this package of ideas called self-concept, I want to relate one final story. It demonstrates what one can do with a good, positive self-concept.

On a beautiful spring day, twenty-five years ago, two young men graduated from the same college. They were very much alike, and both of them were better-than-average students. Both were personable and both were filled with ambitious dreams for the future.

Recently these men returned to their college for their twenty-fifth class reunion. They were still very much alike. Both were happily married, both had three children, and both had gone to work for the same company after graduation. At the time of the reunion, both were still working there.

But there was a difference. One of the men was manager of a small department in that company. The other was its president.

Have you ever wondered, as I have, what makes this kind of difference in people's lives? It can't always be native intelligence or talent or dedication. It can't always be that one person wants success and the other doesn't.

The difference lies in what each person thinks and knows and how he or she makes use of that knowledge. That knowledge consists of two important truths.

First, we need to know that whether a person succeeds or fails is totally determined in his mind. It is determined by his self-confidence and the belief that he can do something.

The second truth is that success and failure are determined by the individual's knowledge and understanding of him or herself. In other words, how you perceive yourself is the hub of the wheel of your life. Your life revolves around your self-concept. The future of your world is in your own mind. You rule over your time, talents, thoughts, and actions. Therefore, self-concept is the number one determining factor of your success or failure.

There are many theories and beliefs about man's creation and how we came to be. But that doesn't concern me now. What concerns me is that from this point on, we create ourselves. We are masters of our own destinies. It is our choice to do what we want with our lives. And what we want should be what we are best-suited for. We must discover ourselves, develop our own individual talents, and strive to become the best we can be at whatever we can do. A singer must sing, an artist must paint, a poet must write if he is to ultimately be at peace with himself. What a man can be, he must be. Remember, no one else can do exactly what you can do. You are unique. Therefore, I dare you to become the best in the world at whatever you can do. You owe it to yourself. Remember, whoever, whatever, and wherever you are, you were born to succeed!

Chapter Eight

"School Is Kool!"

How to Be Successful
Through Academic Achievement

(If you are out of high school, this chapter can still apply.)

The football season was winding down to a close, and the game between the two arch-rival teams was in a few days. Wednesday came, and one football coach found out from the principal that his quarterback and his star running back were ineligible academically. Therefore, the coach called in the best teacher he knew at the school to work with the two boys. "Now, listen," the teacher said, "this is very important. If you two guys don't play on Friday, there's no way we'll ever win. So if you can answer one question correctly, you can be eligible for Friday's game. The question is: Old McDonald had a (blank). Just fill in the blank on your papers. Now I want you to concentrate real hard and think of the answer. I'm going to leave my office, but I'll be back in a few minutes for your papers."

The teacher left, and dead silence filled the room. The quarterback grabbed his head and thought for about five minutes until finally, in desperation, he turned to the running back and asked, "Hey, man, what's the answer? Old McDonald had a what?"

The running back looked at him and said, "Oh man, you dummy! It's easy! Old McDonald had a farm."

The quarterback said, "Oh yeah! That's right! Thanks!

But how do you spell farm?" The running back couldn't believe it but answered anyway, "You dummy, it's easy! E-I-E-I-O."

As you ponder the subtitle of this chapter, "How to Be Successful Through Academic Achievement," I'm sure some of you are wondering, "What does success through academic achievement mean?" And I know, some of you athletes are even wondering, "What in the world does academic mean?" For this reason, this chapter is written to three groups of people: average students, super-achievers, and athletes. I deal with each group in its own section.

The dictionary defines *success* as "attaining a desired object or end. The satisfactory completion of something."

The word *academic* means "of or relating to schools or colleges; literary or general rather than technical; theoretical rather than practical knowledge."

The last word, *achievement,* means "to gain by work or effort." When we put them all together, we have a definition that says, "attaining and completing literary knowledge in school through work and effort." Take time to pick this definition apart so you know you understand it. It's important before you proceed.

Now that I'm out of school and can look back, I realize the years you spend in middle, junior high, and high school are some of the greatest, happiest, and most enjoyable years you'll ever have in your life. At least they can be if you make them that way. There are a lot of good laughs and even some good cries. There are lonely, discouraging times, but there are also great dates, dances, games, study classes, assemblies, dance concerts, music recitals, and parties. All of these activities are fun and they're all part of school.

But as we get caught up in all this excitement, fame, and glory, many of us lose sight of the real reason we go to school. The dances and the football games are fun but they're obviously not the reason we are there. They are a by-product of school. They are called "extracurricular" activities, and they're exactly that. Extra, or in addition to our curriculum, which is schoolwork.

I know it's sometimes hard to remember this, especially when all you're thinking and dreaming about is a date with the "hunk" who sits at the back of your French class, or dinner with that gorgeous, curvy blonde with the nice, big, round eyes who sits in front of you in English. I know school is sometimes hard when you're dreaming about playing college and pro football, being a concert pianist, or being a ballet star. And if any of you are like I was, you're also probably thinking, Hey, how's algebra, typing, history, or English ever going to help me become a better athlete, dancer, or musician? The subjects don't even relate! I don't want to go to school, I just want to be a star!

Well, let me tell you something. Dreams are important. You need to have them, and I want you to continue to dream dreams. But these dreams will never come true if you don't go to school. Besides, there is a direct relationship between math, typing, history, and English and being an athlete, dancer, musician, or teacher.

For example, if an athlete understands math, he can figure out batting averages and work out winning percentages and odds between plays and teams. Dancers can figure out how much to charge for concerts and lessons and how to make a profit. If you understand history and learn how to research, you won't duplicate mistakes of the past in anything you do, and you will be able to find out how to do something the best way before your first attempt. Musicians can take typing, as it limbers up and strengthens hands and fingers, teaches coordination, and develops concentration. And if you understand and master English, your TV interviews will be great when you finally do become a star!

You see, everything in life in some way relates to education and school. That's why it's so important, and that's why it's so important *now*, especially to the average student.

Average Student

It's been said that the chief cause of failure and unhappiness is trading what we want most for what we want at the moment. Think about it! You have to attend classes, pass your classes, achieve some sort of grade-point average, and graduate from high school if you ever plan on achieving your other goals and dreams. It's all part of the game of life and is required by our society. It's not required to hassle you but to help you become the best you can be.

Therefore, don't fight it — it won't hurt you to accept it and go with the flow. You've got to remember that you wouldn't even have a dance club, football team, jazz band, debate team, ski club, or student body officers, for that matter, if there wasn't a school to attend. School is the reason you can enjoy these great experiences. Therefore, academic achievement comes first. Right now it's supposed to! All other activities are extracurricular and must come second, third, and so on, on your priority list.

You don't know how lucky we are to live in America and be able to go to school. Everyone in America has the opportunity to attend school, but in many other countries in the world, they don't even have schools!

In Afghanistan, for instance, did you know that 90 percent of the population can't even read? And yet in America we have Evelyn Wood and all the other speed reading courses where we can learn to read hundreds of words a minute! We are so lucky here — but for some reason, many young people don't realize it. They waste time and don't take advantage of their current chance for an education.

Education is the most prized possession on earth! In fact, if you believe in life after death, you'll understand that education is an eternal principle and it is the only thing you can take with you when you die. An unknown author stresses the importance and significance of education with this definition:

> Education is a companion which no misfortune can de-
> crease, no crime destroy, no enemy alienate, no despotism
> enslave; at home a friend, abroad an introduction, in solitude
> a solace, in society an ornament. It chastens life, guides
> virtue, and gives grace and government to genius.
> Education may cost financial sacrifice and mental pain, but
> in both money and life's values, it will repay every cost one-
> hundredfold.

Academic Success Is Simple

I've only been out of junior high and high school a few short years, and as I look back, which is an easy way to learn what to do and what not to do if given a second chance, I realize the fundamental thing I've discovered about achieving academic success is that it's simple! It took me awhile, but I finally discovered that while we're in school, all areas of our lives must revolve around school. They have to! If they don't, we'll fall behind and eventually fail, not only in school but also in life.

That's what happened to me — I wish I could have read a book like this one, or had someone point out the tragic consequences of my actions and warn me to change long before I did. I missed many opportunities and wasted much time as a result of it.

There's a big transition in going from junior high to high school, and I got caught up in it. My story starts when I was fifteen, in my first year of the "big time" high school. All I could think about was playing high school and college football, basketball, and baseball. I knew I had to play these sports if I was to someday fulfill my dream to be a professional athlete. So I thought only about sports. Sure, I started out the year hitting most of my classes to keep me eligible, but as the year progressed, I soon got caught up in being cool and conceited, and I missed class a few times to do some things with the boys. Consequently, I fell further and further behind the other students. I started being late for school, I didn't do my homework at night, and I was unprepared for several classes. Now I really didn't want to go to class for fear I would be called on, so I sluffed them. And the rut just got deeper and deeper. How was I supposed to concentrate on pursuing my other goals when I knew I was flunking out of school? What would my parents think? How would it affect my athletics? How would it affect my getting a job?

It wasn't until I got caught sluffing and got into trouble that I finally changed. It happened when I called my teacher at school one day and said, "Dan Clark is sick and can't attend class today. He requested me to notify you." The teacher answered, "All right. Who is this speaking?" And, like an idiot I replied, "This is my father." Believe me, sluffing and trying to be cool isn't worth it!

You see what can happen virtually overnight if you don't put academic achievement first? If your schoolwork isn't done, nothing else of worth will get done, either. You can't perform to the best of your ability in sports, music, drama, debate, or anything else if you don't have the peace of mind that you have when you know your schoolwork is under control.

Keep Schoolwork Under Control

How do you get your schoolwork under control? It's simple! You do your homework on time and go to bed at night on time so you can wake up on time to eat a good breakfast on time and make it to your first class on time. And when you start off on time on the right foot, the other steps will usually fall into place. Doing your schoolwork and attending class the rest of the day will then flow smoothly. Even your extracurricular activities will go better because you'll be able to totally concentrate on what you're doing and not worry about what you haven't done.

Another advantage that comes to you and your friends as you attend your classes is that you won't have time to get into trouble with the law or with your boyfriend or girlfriend. Statistics tell us these problems occur mostly while young people are sluffing classes. In other words, problems occur because the students are doing something they should not be doing when they should not be doing it. Think about this and commit to do what you're supposed to do. It's your choice — no one can force you to do it! It's totally up to you. Organized and successful or chaotic and abusive — which cycle do you want to guide your life?

Don't Ever Drop Out

If you want to become the best you can be, it all depends on how serious you take your education. It's dependent upon whether or not you go to school, attend class when you should, and learn as much as you possibly can while you're there. Remember, you have to graduate from junior high to get to high school, and you *must* have a high school diploma if you want to go somewhere and be somebody in life. High school graduation is a symbol of academic achievement, and it must be accomplished. Why put in eight or nine years of school to get into high school and then throw it all away because you don't hang in there long enough to graduate?

The dropout rate in America is a national disgrace. The rate in some city schools is as high as 40 to 50 percent, with 33 percent dropping out at the sophomore level. Why do students drop out? It's because school is a drag. And why is school a drag? Because they've made it that way. They've missed classes and explanations. Consequently they don't understand, fall behind, feel the pressure of making up the work, and decide to "bag" the whole thing.

If you're thinking about dropping out of school because you're disenchanted, don't do it! I guarantee that one day you'll regret it. Don't run from your problems; stand up and face them. Start by going to your counselor and teacher and talking to them. Tell them you're behind the other students (which will be no surprise to them), and that you would like to do what is necessary to catch up. It won't be easy. You may even have to sacrifice some social activities for a while until you've caught up. But whatever is required of you, do it. It will definitely be worth your while! You'll never regret all the benefits and rich rewards that will come to you from achieving academic success and graduating from high school.

I know that getting a tutor and talking with all these folks sounds uncool and that you're probably worried about what your friends might think. But I'm telling you, it's worth going through whatever it takes. Besides, your friends and their negative influence on you are the major cause of your problems in the first place. You've spent so much time with them that you've missed out on other important things — namely, achieving in school.

Hey, now it's time to be a little bit selfish and start spending some time on you — some time just helping and bettering you!

You and your welfare are a lot more important than anything else in the world right now. Think about how short your school days are as compared to how long you'll have to think about the consequences if you fail in life because you blew your education as a kid. Put yourself five or ten years ahead and look back to see if what you're doing now is harmful or helpful to your future happiness and welfare.

If I've sufficiently convinced you to care enough about

yourself to change, and if you do what I'm suggesting, then don't worry about what anyone thinks. Remember, you're getting back into the swing of things for you. You're doing it to bring yourself up to the high level of achievement you can and deserve to attain. Go for it! You have nothing to lose and everything to gain.

Super-Achievers

Just as important as those individuals who miss class and underachieve are those of you who are great and conscientious students — the super-achievers. What about you? Many of you are thinking, Why am I even reading this chapter? I have a 3.5 grade-point average, I'm on the honor roll, I'm student body president, captain of the basketball team, soloist in the choir, and just an all-around wonderful person. I'm already motivated and accomplishing a lot. Why are you talking to me?

The answer is simple. Life is not a destination, it's a journey. Accomplishments are springboards for more accomplishments. Just because a person has achieved success doesn't give him or her a license to retire. A great deal of study has been done on retired people, and the results are quite conclusive. True retirement means death. Studies clearly show that those individuals who are looking forward to retiring and doing nothing after many years of hard work usually live less than seven years. If they don't have something else in mind — another goal to keep them going — they have nothing to live for and soon die.

What does this have to do with you as a young super-achiever? I've interviewed a lot of youth leaders and honor students who have achieved a great deal in certain areas of their lives, and I've found that many of you outstanding students are definitely in retirement. You're just cruising through school with little effort in areas that come easy and no effort at all in areas that present a problem. Many of you are great in math and science, but lousy in sports or art. Some of you are great in woodshop and in auto mechanics, but you're terrible in English. Consequently, you spend all of your time at things that you're good at, the things that come easy. You're retired from setting new goals for yourself and are just cruising in a holding pattern, not

139

becoming the best you can be.

If this group doesn't include you, then perhaps you are retired in a different sense. You have accomplished high goals in one field, but instead of continuing with your achivements, you go into retirement and live off your past laurels. You become complacent and say, "I've been on the honor roll. I've received 100 on a math test." You act like because you've done it once, you don't have to keep up the good work and do it again. You're in the same situation as the Olympic champion who wins the gold medal and stands on the pedestal in all his proud glory as the "Star-Spangled Banner" plays. This poses two questions: Can he stay on the pedestal forever or does he have to come down? And when he comes down, can he live off that moment of glory forever or does he have to set another goal and accomplish it? I feel I can safely say that when he comes down and tries to live off that moment for too long, he will fade away and accomplish nothing more for the rest of his life. But if he looks at his gold medal accomplishment as a way to help him achieve his next higher goal, he can reflect on his past success for motivation and encouragement as he sets out to accomplish his new goal. Super-achievers — don't be retired; be inspired to do something more!

Too many outstanding students are satisfied with getting an A on a test or report card rather than striving to learn as much as they possibly can. For them, an A is easy to get. It doesn't come as a result of long hours of study and hard work and is taken for granted.

Getting an A is fine. But you'll notice, I didn't say *achieving* it. To achieve something means to gain by work or effort. Therefore, to be successful, one must achieve and expend real effort. Now you tell me, if someone gets an A grade without expending effort, is he really academically successful?

The next time you receive an A, ask yourself, "Did I achieve it or just get it. Did I do my very best?" And if you feel you did your very best, then do more! Ask yourself, "Could I invent a mathematics theorem and write a paper on it? Could I go beyond the classroom requirements and do something extra special?" Don't be content with your present circumstances — you can improve them! If your grade-point average is 3.5, don't just maintain it; make it better. If it's 4.0, then maintain it by continuing to set challenging goals, but don't stop there. Start improving other areas of your life and make them 4.0 as well!

Athletes

Before we move on, I need to talk to one more group of individuals — the athletes, both men and women. To me, sports competition is life personified; it is the essence of what life is all about. I believe that it's extremely important for every individual to engage in competition during his lifetime, and I feel that sports competition is the best kind. I didn't say we have to be athletes to be somebody — I just mean we can learn so much about success in life from sports competition!

Because athletic competition is so exciting and rewarding, we sometimes get so wrapped up in it that we tend to lose sight of the other important areas in our lives. We lose proper perspective and make sports instead of schoolwork our number one priority. We don't realize how much we're messing up our athletic future by not studying or going to class. At the beginning of the season we haven't received our first report card, so we haven't yet been told about our poor classroom performance. Getting our picture in the sports section means more to us than getting an A on a math test. But by the end of the season, when college recruiters start wanting to draft us into their athletic programs, suddenly pictures, publicity, and statistics don't mean as much. I know — it happened to me!

If you don't have a reasonable grade-point average, and I mean at least a 2.5, most college coaches will just check you off their list. It's not their choice; it's an NCAA rule. Many of them can't even get you admitted into their school if you don't have a certain GPA. And don't get it by cheating! I remember overhearing two basketball players talking during a math test. One asked the other, "How far are you from the correct answer?" The other player answered, "About two seats away!"

A nationwide NCAA rule regarding college football teams states that only thirty new players can be given scholarships each year. Think about the thousands of high school players you're competing against just to be recruited. Now you answer this one: If a coach has a choice between two players of comparable athletic potential and ability, and one is going to class and maintaining a good GPA and the other is sluffing school and has a low GPA, which player is the college recruiter going to select?

I didn't know for sure, so I interviewed ten major college coaches. The results were overwhelming. Regardless of the outstanding physical ability of the two players being recruited, ten out of ten coaches would select the student athlete over the I-don't-care-about-school athlete. The reason was also unanimous. Ten out of ten coaches said that if a guy or girl isn't responsible enough to go to class, he or she won't be responsible enough to play the sport. If athletes won't study English and math like they're required to do, they won't study and learn the defensive formations or offensive plays like they're supposed to do. The coaches also commented that athletes who won't go to class and do the work will never be players anyway, because they will never be academically eligible to play. Just because you're on campus and enrolled in school doesn't mean you've "got it made in the shade." If an athlete won't go to class and stay eligible in high school, he or she probably won't stay eligible in college, either. The coaches can't afford to take the chance of wasting one of their precious scholarships on anyone who'll never be eligible to play. If you're in this situation, it's not too late! You *can* change your bad habits. You *can* change your academic situation. The choice is yours.

Please listen to me and don't think you're so "bad" in sports that school doesn't matter. It really, truly, honestly does! You can no longer get into a university and be just a "dumb jock." These days, you have to be a *student athlete*.

You Succeed with Your Attitude

Now that each of you knows why you should achieve academically, let's look at the "how to." The "how to" is called "attitude," which we've already discussed in Chapter 6.

Positive mental attitude, or PMA as it's called, is talked about a lot, but it's rarely discussed when the conversation is about school or academic achievement. You see, when you're playing football or writing a paper or playing a trumpet or dancing on stage, people will always tell you, "You can do it if you think you can. Just practice and have a positive mental attitude and you can do anything." But when you're working on math or chemistry problems, how many times have you heard somebody say, "You can do it if you just think positively"? I've never heard anyone say it! Everyone always tells me mathematics is an exact science. Everyone knows that 2+2=4 and 8x9=72, and regardless if you think positively or negatively, the answer will always be the same.

But this just isn't so. Having a proper positive attitude is essential to our success in all areas of life, including academic achievement. Sure, mathematics is an exact science. Two plus two equals four, but this is not where PMA comes into play.

What if someone gives you a more complicated problem, one that would require hours of concentrated, trial-and-error hard work to solve? And what if the person giving you the equation swears there is no answer, assuring you it's impossible? They tell you not even Einstein could solve it! Do you think you would even try to solve it? I don't think many of us would. Why? Because we have a negative attitude!

On the other hand, people who believed positively that there was a way to solve a tricky problem hung in there, sometimes for years. Albert Einstein, Thomas Edison, Dr. Melvin Cook, and many more proved the importance of PMA — even in mathematics.

Let me tell you a quick story about a similar situation when the outcome was much different than it might have been because those involved had a positive attitude. It involves PMA in the academic world.

I was one of 104 young men and women who were given a 250-page script with the assignment to memorize it in sixty to ninety days. Every *the, and,* and *but* had to be perfect in order to pass the test. When I opened the book and began to study it, I told myself, "This is impossible! This leader is nuts! This assignment is crazy! No one could ever memorize this tiny printed script and pass it off verbatim.

And if they could, it certainly would take longer than two or three months."

I wasn't the only one with a negative attitude, but we didn't have much say in the matter, so we began to chisel away at this impossible task. Every day we heard positive reinforcement and positive "it's-possible — you-can-do-it" statements from the leaders. And do you know what? The negative impossibilities became positive possibilities and most of the 104 passed the test with word-perfect memorization in the ninety days.

Several months passed, and I found myself in a leadership role responsible to see that four different young men and women memorize the same script in the same time frame. However, because of my belief in PMA, and an urge to prepare them sooner, I thought they could do it in less than sixty days. As a matter of fact, I knew they could do it in twenty days. I wrote up a new program schedule, showed them how to do it, and committed these "impossible" negative people to become positive thinkers.

The results were astonishing! Not only did all four people pass off the script in twenty days, but, during the next year, almost one hundred men and women passed off the same script in the now-required twenty days. And as the skeptical negative thoughts eventually turned to positive beliefs, the days to do this decreased until a girl from Scotland passed off the script in ten days.

Now you tell me, does having a positive attitude have an effect on our success in academic achievement? You bet it does! Attitude is the name of the game! Even in school, if you think you can, you can.

As we draw this topic to a close, there's one more definition of academic achievement that must be discussed. To me, achieving academically implies more than attending school and getting good grades. It implies that some degree of education and learning has taken place. In other words, going to class is a start, but it's not enough. Why not get educated? *Education* is defined as "to develop and cultivate mentally and morally. To receive training, discipline, schooling, and instruction."

Our success in life is not dependent just on our class attendance and ability to get an A. It's much more than

144

that. Success comes only as we learn something, only as new knowledge is constantly obtained. When we obtain knowledge, we must use it, not just store it. A lot of people know a lot about a lot of things, but they very seldom practice what they know or preach. I've spoken to groups when people start smiling or begin nodding their heads in agreement as I speak. They imply that they already know everything about what I'm saying. This occasionally frustrates me and tempts me to stop speaking and ask, "Okay, sure you agree with me, but what have you done about the things I'm saying?" Until you do something with what you've learned, your knowledge will do you no good. The person who can read but won't is no better off than the person who doesn't know how. Schooling leads to education, but it's a far cry from the end result. Schooling is what teaches people to read, but education is when they actually have learned by reading.

This also explains the difference between intelligence or knowledge, and education. Everyone has some degree of intelligence. Everyone has the potential to learn and increase in knowledge. But very few are educated. You see, education is applied knowledge. It's the ability to put knowledge into action. If someone is educated, it implies that they not only *know*, but they can also *do*.

Remember, then, that the key to your success is not merely a degree and schooling, but education. All things revolve around it and are guaranteed by it. This is why success comes in all areas of life through academic achievement. It's the ground floor, the fundamental foundation area of life that we must excel in if we are to live a happy, free, and successful life. Sure, we were born to succeed, but without education and academic achievement, we'll never make it! Because our generation of young Americans is soon to be the leaders of society, we must make a commitment to excellence in education now. The future of the world is dependent on us, and we can't let ourselves or our friends down!

Chapter Nine

"Why Get High?"

How to Refrain from Drugs, Alcohol, and Committing Suicide

A man had a dream one night and the principles he learned in that dream apply to all of us. He relates: "I dreamed that I had done something great. In recognition of my service, an angel appeared and said he would grant any wish I desired. After contemplating the possibilities, I decided to ask him for love, peace, and happiness to fill the whole earth. In response to my wish, the angel answered, 'That's good, sir, but we don't deal in fruits here; we only deal in seeds.'" The dream ended.

Deal with "Seeds," Not "Fruits," of Problems

This is true in real life. All of us need to deal with seeds as the single solution to every problem we encounter. But when you think about it, doesn't our society concentrate more on problems than on solutions to the problems? If we are ever going to change and make a better world for ourselves, we need to dig through the fruits of failures and find the seeds that cause them.

Alcohol, drunk driving, drug abuse, and suicide are all fruits. They come as a result of actions caused by bad seeds. Alcohol and drugs are not the real problems. The problems

and solutions rest in the question, Why are kids doing what they're doing? All of our emphasis, time, and talents seem to be spent on the rehabilitation of bad fruits instead of working with preventative measures at the seed level.

What is this "seed" level we're referring to? It's nothing more than the seeds this book is getting you to plant and nurture. If we want to clean up our world and rid it of these rotten fruits (not the people — just their bad habits), all we need to do is develop a good self-concept, develop self-discipline, decide on some goals, and learn to communicate to receive counsel from our families.

As we young people are growing up and weaving our way through life, each of us is faced with fulfilling three basic needs: the need to feel love; the need to feel wanted and important; and the need to feel a true sense of security. As needy humans, we will do almost anything to satisfy these three basic wants. We'll change our dress codes, alter our moral characters, compromise on habits and beliefs, and change nearly anything we have to in order to fulfill these needs. It's sad but it's true!

Communicating at Home

This is why communication at home is so important. Because we're talking about seeds and causes of bad fruits, let's break down our needs and the apparent timetable of fulfillment. Before a child is ten years old he or she has a strong need for love. After eighteen, it's a strong need for security. But between ten and eighteen years of age, the average person seeks to fulfill the need to feel wanted and important. And in so doing, he or she usually does what he or she has to do to get attention.

Picture this: A young girl comes into the kitchen to show her mother a nice picture she's drawn for her. In response, her mother smiles, takes the picture, praises her for her wonderful work, hangs it on the refrigerator door, and says, "Thank you." She makes a big deal out of her work. Obviously, the girl feels wanted and important and feels like doing more of the same to get this much-needed attention. So she does! And by so doing she stays out of trouble and mischief and becomes a noble citizen. She grows up believing recognition and feelings of importance come by doing good things.

In contrast, picture this: A young boy comes into the kitchen to show his mother the picture he drew. In response, she says, "That's nice, but don't bother me now — I'm cooking." To this, the boy leaves not satisfied, not feeling wanted and important, and not having his need for attention fulfilled. So he tries another way — Plan B. He goes into the hall and writes on the walls with a crayon. He goes back into the kitchen for attention but still receives a cold shoulder. Now, in desperation, he decides to break a window. At least it makes noise and will cause something to happen! And, sure enough, it does. Mother doesn't have time to praise his good work, but for some reason, she has time to punish him. She is furious, grabs him, spanks him, and calls Dad, who now scolds him and punishes him too. Sure, the kid gets his needed attention, but something is still missing that he doesn't realize until this episode is over. He still doesn't feel wanted and important at home. This hurts him and confuses him further. So, to satisfy this very strong desire, the young boy goes elsewhere — to his circle of friends. He first tries the "straight" guys, but they don't make a fuss over him. Now, with nowhere else to go, he turns his needs to other sources — the wild bunch! After a while, because he can guzzle as much as the big boys can, blow smoke rings, is funny when he's drunk, and always has the best "pot" in school, he feels cool, wanted, and important.

Can you see what happened? Review the two examples again. This doesn't just happen to young children! If people at any age are praised for good actions and complimented when they achieve wholesome goals, they will continue to pursue wholesome ambitions and habits. On the other hand, if people don't receive recognition for worthwhile endeavors and are recognized instead for breaking the law or breaking their health, which are they going to continue doing? Think about it and get your parents and friends to think about it. Review your own personal experiences and examine your past sources of attention. I'm sure you'll agree it's true!

When a young adult can get attention from the seeds of doing good and wholesome things, alcohol and drugs will no longer be needed and used. When young people find out who they are and what they represent, and then set high goals to become the best they can be, they will perform healthy deeds in reality and won't take drugs to go to "dreamland." They will have solutions to their problems, so they won't have to take a quick remedy drink, pill, or puff to handle them. They will know at all times what they are doing, feel better about themselves physically, mentally, and emotionally, and will truly satisfy their need to feel wanted and important.

When we sow the seeds of a good self-concept, cultivate the self-discipline necessary to say no to filthy fruits, and nurture some lofty goals, we will attain powerful inner strength, and our world will reap the fruits of love, peace, and happiness as was requested in the man's dream I mentioned at the beginning of this chapter.

A good story which demonstrates this is about Aladdin, a poor Chinese boy who became king of Persia. His story began when an African magician hired Aladdin to go into an underground cave for a magic lamp. When he found it, he accidently rubbed the lamp, and the genie, the spirit of the lamp, appeared. This powerful spirit, which became the slave of the person who possessed the lamp, granted Aladdin's every wish. Aladdin married the sultan's daughter, and the genie built them a wonderful palace. But the wicked magician tracked them down, tricked the princess into trading the old lamp for a new one, and transported the whole palace to Africa. Aladdin followed the magician there, regained the lamp, and restored the palace to China.

Many people, since that story was originally told, have wished for some way to call on extra power to get them what they want. And this quest for power and personal success is still one of the strongest desires known to man. Each of us does some daydreaming about how convenient it would be to have a dependable, personal genie always at our elbow to help solve our problems and get us what we want.

Our Inner "Genie"

Sure, we don't have a real genie as Aladdin did, but what we do not often realize is that we do have an unbelievable power, our spirit, at our command, which we allow to go largely unutilized. We don't have to look elsewhere. The power is within us. Therefore, we, as young people, need to do some soul-searching and screw our heads on straight — we need to discover our unbelievable power "genie" within us and use it in our efforts to sow the seeds of success. We need to stop making excuses for using alcohol and drugs and start doing what we want to do and should be doing! The greatest source of power, now as anciently, is in people! It has been estimated that the average man still uses only a small fraction of his potential. They say our powers go unused. I disagree! Our powers only go undiscovered and misunderstood. The thing that we probably know the least about is our own individual selves. We know how to fly faster than sound and how to build almost anything to promote comfort. We have solved our problems of food supply, housing, transportation, and communication. We have even reached into the world of the atom. Yet we still don't know how to control our moods, our enthusiasm, our passions, our tempers, or our thoughts.

Deep down inside, thousands of people want to do right, but instead they are doing things that shock and embarrass families, friends, and themselves. Many are going to psychiatrists to ask why, and even psychiatrists are wondering why they do as they do. But no one seems to know why! Without overstepping my bounds, I think I do — let me explain and show you how you can always do the things you know you should do and want to do.

Living somewhere in the unexplored regions of the mind is a wonderfully efficient helper who can transform lives. When fully commissioned, he is a marvel of accomplishment. This is our genie. It took Aladdin quite a while to discover the power of his genie, and it may also take a while to understand and discover the power within us. You see, man is a contradictory being. We have both virtue and vice intermingled within us. It often is an internal "civil war." H. G. Wells described this when he said, "I am not a man but a mob." He understood that

151

within us is an entire population that sometimes gets going in a dozen different directions at the same time. When this happens, we become stalemated and confused. We no longer know what we want to do and end up doing what others are doing. This is how we create habits we don't particularly want.

To halt this from happening, remember that a group of workers will always get more done if you make the best worker — the most desirable one — the boss in charge of the others. Do this in your mind. Choose the best thought, the most virtuous habit, and make it the boss to rule over your other feelings. Like workers, the mind can be given extra authority and charged with additional power. Instead of being pushed around by the appetites, passions, fears, and doubts that support our less desirable selves, the best thought, goal, and desire in the mind will reign supreme. We have great authority and control over our arms and legs. When we tell them to move, they obey. We can also exercise that same kind of authority over our tongues, hearts, ambitions, and bad habits. By wisely marshalling our powers we can avoid anything, stop anything, and always do exactly what we want to do. Therefore, let's sow the seeds of success; the seeds of a positive mental attitude; the seeds of a good self-concept.

Now that you understand the powers you possess to help stop the bad fruits of failure, let me give you some motivation to help you begin doing something about them today. The following are true accounts and statistics of the consequences and bad experiences resulting from alcohol, drug abuse, and suicide. Think about them. Better still, let them into your heart and feel them. Then, commit to doing something about changing these tragic trends that are literally killing our country.

"Big Apple" Is Stoned

One out of every forty New York City residents is a heroin addict, making the city the heroin capital of the nation, reports United Press International.

The study, conducted by former Health, Education, and Welfare Secretary Joseph Califano, Jr., and released in 1982, showed the number of heroin addicts is up 50 percent in three years.

Califano said addiction to heroin and other drugs such as cocaine, alcohol, and cigarette smoking has become America's number one health problem. And notice the four he grouped together. You can't learn to smoke pot until you've learned to smoke cigarettes, which indicates pot smoking stems from cigarette smoking! Because this is true, could excessive alcohol usage lead to cocaine and heroin usage, that "easier-than-alcohol" way to get high? You bet it can!

Califano's report, which covered the years 1978 through 1981, showed there were between 450,000 and 600,000 heroin addicts in the United States, or one out of every seventy-five U.S. residents.

Something must be done! You know that the seeds of success must first be planted in order to bring about change. Take the responsibility upon yourself and go for it!

A Judge's Lecture

Recently, a seventeen-year-old Florida boy pleaded guilty to possessing hallucinogenic drugs. He had also been charged with violence toward a Miami Beach police officer.

Judge Alfonso Sepe sentenced the youth to one year in the county stockade and four years of probation.

The following is the judge's lecture given to the boy in the presence of his grieving parents. It was published in the "Dear Abby" newspaper column.

> Judge Sepe spoke directly to the youth and said, "Do you know who is going to serve that year? Not you; your mother and father will serve that year.
>
> "That is what's wrong. *They* get sentenced! They get sentences for a lifetime while you serve a year. Your body is in the stockade for a year, but their souls are tormented for a lifetime. Why? Because you are a selfish, spoiled boy, that's why!
>
> "There is no punishment in the world that I could inflict upon you that could in any way compensate for what you are doing to your mother and father. I have not spent five cents raising you. I didn't know you from Adam. But your mother and father have put their lives, their hearts, their sweat, their money, and everything else they have into bringing you up. And now they have to sit in this courtroom and listen to a

total stranger who had nothing to do with your upbringing scold you and put you in jail.

"This is at a time when phony kids your age are yelling, 'You adults have your alcohol, we want our drugs; you have polluted our water and our air, you have polluted this and that'; and all the rest of the garbage that comes out of your mouths.

"Meanwhile, you put yourselves above everybody else. I feel sorry for you.

"I want you to think of this for one year, and the reason why I say it:

"If you are sick, a doctor will treat you and he won't be on drugs. The lawyer who represents you won't be high on drugs, and the people in whose custody you'll be won't be on drugs.

"Your astronauts are not on drugs, and your President is not, and your legislators are not.

"And your engineers who build the bridges that you drive across and the tunnels that you drive through are not on drugs, and those who build the planes that you fly in and the cars that you drive are not.

"Neither are those who build the bathrooms that you stink up with your lousy, rotten drugs.

"None of them have been on drugs, and this is because of people like your mother and father.

"But in the world of the future," Sepe went on, "the same may not be true. Teachers, doctors, lawyers, legislators — products of the new drug-oriented generation — may well be high as kites.

"You won't know whom to send your child to, or whom to trust your life to."

Sepe sighed and closed the case file.

"Let's see what kind of world you leave to your children," he said, "before you talk about the world that we left to ours."

Alcohol and Drunk Driving

In July of 1982, a handsome young man, seventeen years old, intelligent, hard-working, and recently elected student body president at his high school, was driving with his beautiful sixteen-year-old girlfriend — scholar, dancer and cheerleader. They were on their way home from a fun-filled date. At 11:15 p.m. they were going east on a busy street. I'm sure they were laughing and talking, maybe holding hands, with the radio playing a favorite tune, when it happened. A man driving under the influence of alcohol ran a red light and with that increased speed, ran the next red light going south and plowed into the students' car. It was a small car and the innocent kids were thrown many feet from the point of the collision, dying an instant, unnecessary death.

There were thousands of sorrowful, sobbing young friends and parents attending each of the young student's funerals. And all anyone could feel or wonder was Why? It was so tragic and unnecessary and senseless.

I'm sure you're wondering what happened to the stupid idiot driving the other car. Well, this drunken fool suffered only a few minor cuts and scratches and was released from the hospital. It was reported that when the doctor in the emergency room asked him if he realized what he had done, the drunk replied, "I don't give a damn what I've done!" The sad part about his story is that he had already been picked up twice for drunk driving and had a suspended license, but he had never been cited. His hands were barely slapped legally, and he was let go. He never should have been driving — ever — especially that tragic summer night!

For those of you who drink alcohol or know someone else who drinks, note that I'm not criticizing the performer, I'm criticizing the performance! It is downright stupid to drive when you drink — even a little bit! Five people I knew in high school were killed as a result of drunk driving. They were seventeen-year-old guys who had so much to live for. Something should be done in our court systems to punish and stop drunk driving — something more than is now being done! Lifetime imprisonment? No driving privileges ever again? Death penalty when someone is killed? You laugh and say, "Relax, buddy, you're coming down kind of hard." Well, what if the one who gets killed by a drunk driver is your young brother or your best friend? Think about some solutions!

In the United States each year, fifty thousand people are killed and two million seriously injured as a result of drunk driving. According to the National Highway Traffic Safety Administration, about half of our nation's traffic deaths are related to alcohol abuse.

Eighty percent of fatal accidents are first accidents. This figure underscores one of the most tragic parts of today's grim picture: those at greatest risk are our youth. In 1980, the U.S. Surgeon General revealed that although the overall death rate for every other age group dropped in the period between 1970 and 1978, the death rate for fifteen- to twenty-four-year-olds rose. Today nearly half of all teenage deaths are due to motor vehicle accidents, and most of these involve either drunk driving or marijuana use.

Think about this: statistics tell us that each man, woman, and child in the United States can expect to be in a car crash once every ten years. With the constant rise of alcohol and drug users driving while they're "wasted," our chances go up considerably! Because any of us can be "hit" at any time by this alarming fact, it behooves us greatly to do what we can to arrest this menace called "death on the highways." You know what the seeds are that must be planted in order to bring about the change. Take the responsibility upon yourself and do something about it.

I've been affected by alcohol during my life in so many ways that, personally, I don't understand why young people want to drink alcohol. Evangeline Booth wrote:

> Drink has shed more blood, hung more crepe, sold more homes, plunged more people into bankruptcy, armed more villains, slain more children, snapped more wedding rings, defiled more innocence, blinded more eyes, dethroned more reason, wrecked more manhood, dishonored more womanhood, broken more hearts, blasted more lives, driven more to suicide, and dug more graves than any other scourge that has cursed the world.

So why do people drink? They say these horrible things I've mentioned would never happen to them, but why do they even take the chance? I found this article, "Ten Reasons Why I Drink," that finally answers the question. If you drink, don't feel you're too cool or macho to put up with this. Just read it and think about what it's saying. Remember, I'm not criticizing the performer — only the performance!

"Ten Reasons Why I Drink"

1. I love to vomit.
2. (Men) It makes my family respect me. I want to win the girlfriend-beating, friend-fighting, child-abuse championship of the world.

3. (Women) It makes me feel good the next morning when I know things happened that shouldn't have happened, and I was taken advantage of.

4. It helps me prove that I'm coordinated and can stumble gracefully.

5. It helps me win the safe-driving award. People love for me to kill their innocent sons and daughters.

6. It proves that man can become a cow. The only difference between a man and a cow is man's ability to reason. When I drink, I lose my ability to reason and am no better off than a cow.

7. It helps me stay awake all night to study because I was too busy to study when I should have.

8. It helps me to spend my money on fun instead of my important bills.

9. It helps me to realize my dream of living in an alley on Skid Row when my girlfriend, and eventually my wife and children, leave me.

10. It is truly my way of getting rid of my problems, facing them like a real man or a woman would, solving them, and never having to face them again.

Because hard-line surveys and in-depth research show that you have to learn how to smoke cigarettes before you can learn to smoke marijuana which in turn could lead to usage of "harder" drugs; because cigarette smoking is a definite drug addiction; and because I already listed reasons why people drink, I thought you might be interested in another article, the list of reasons why people smoke. Again, don't be offended — just think about the overall message of this chapter.

"Ten Reasons Why I Smoke"

1. It's such a clean, refined habit. I love to cough and spit.

2. It makes my breath so pleasing to everyone. Kissing me is like licking an ashtray.

3. It sets a good example for children and friends to follow.

4. It makes my teeth and fingers so pretty and yellow, and makes my clothes, car, and house smell so clean and fresh.

5. It proves I have self-control, that I'm not a slave to anything.

6. I want to see how much poison my body can take in before I die — and maybe that isn't too far away.

7. It's fun to throw my "cigs" out the window and litter, start forest fires, and kill wildlife and nature.

8. (Men) It means I'm tough and rugged and able to ride a horse in a cow pasture at sunset.

9. (Women) It tells everyone I'm wild and ready for a good time. I like to abuse my body, so why don't you do it, too.

10. It is my way of showing people how secure I feel, that I'm not nervous, that I like myself, and that I have a desire to take care of my health because others are counting on me.

Suicide and Depression

In a small town in northern New Jersey in December 1979, two sixteen-year-old high school boys — classmates in an affluent community — hanged themselves within a few days of each other. The summer before, a twelve-year-old girl in the same community ended her short life with an overdose of aspirin. And a year earlier, a short distance away, another teen-age boy killed himself. In another part of America, a six-year-old girl had a fight with her mother and attempted suicide with her grandmother's diet pills. In an affluent West Coast area, a well-known TV personality lost his daughter when she committed suicide after overdosing with LSD. Around the corner from my home in Salt Lake City, a beautiful young girl got involved with a guy, slipped up and got pregnant, was rejected at home, couldn't handle the pressure, and died from an overdose of sleeping pills. And finally, in the small town of Pine Ridge, South Dakota, something very tragic happened in the 1970s. In one of the high schools, ninety-six freshmen entered the ninth grade. By the time six years had passed (two years after graduation), forty-two of the ninety-six students were dead. Every death was suicide — either alcohol or drug related!

This tragic list could go on and on and sadly on! More than 400,000 young people from ages fifteen to twenty-four attempt suicide each year, and more than 10,000 of them are successful. Thirty young students kill themselves each day! It appears we are in the midst of an epidemic of teenage suicides, for among youngsters age ten to nineteen, the rate of suicide has tripled since the late 1950s. Suicides are up 92 percent in the last two years! Among the fifteen-to nineteen-year-olds alone, the rate has doubled since the late 1960s. Suicide is the third leading cause of death of fifteen-to twenty-four year olds. (The two leading causes are accidents and homocides.)

Young suiciders are junior-high, high-school, or college teenagers; they include both drop-outs and graduates from all financial, educational, and ethnic racial backgrounds. Suicide affects everyone! In fact, psychiatrists and psychologists tell us everyone contemplates suicide at some time in his or her life. But why? Why do people get depressed and discouraged to the point where they want to end it all?

The answer is: they don't have a basic philosophy of life! They are not aware of the seeds of success that they can develop to overcome depression. We truly need to be aware of these people; they can be friends, relatives, or perhaps even ourselves. We need to stop them, love them, and help them help themselves. According to Dr. Mary Griffin, a Chicago psychiatrist, most of those who commit suicide are desperate for help and don't know where or how to find it. The cry for help is sent out to "significant others." These are the key people in that young person's life — family members, friends, or sometimes a teacher. Usually the suicide attempt is made only when all communication lines with these "significant others" have finally broken down. This is why it's extremely important for us to dig in now and help ourselves and our fellowmen to feel love, importance, and security.

Warning signs of suicidal behavior are important to know. Listed below are the major signs:

1. Suicide threats.

2. Preoccupation with death.

3. Recent loss of a loved one, accompanied by feelings of loneliness and guilt.

4. Family disruptions that cause an abrupt change of personality and behavior.

5. Impulsiveness and impatience; a low level of tolerance for anything.

If you recognize any of these signs in others or perhaps notice them creeping into your life, do something to make that individual or yourself feel loved, wanted, important, and secure. Help him to overcome his anxiety. Be his sincere friend. Start working on helping him plant the seeds of success that we've discussed.

The last and possibly the most devastating behavioral suicidal sign to look for and react to is:

6. Depression — both mild and severe.

Depression is known by many different names and is recognized by many different symptoms. It affects each person uniquely and in many different ways.

Depression is common — all of us have experienced it at one time or another by feeling temporarily not needed, lonely, "bummed out," or too tired to care. This type of depression affects us occasionally and is regularly overcome. But what about those people who experience it constantly? For them, depression is a serious challenge that requires an effort just to get through the hours of a day. They firmly believe other's problems may be solvable, but not theirs. They believe they are stuck forever.

If you're in this category and you realize it, you are already half cured. Recognizing a problem in yourself is not a "bad scene" — it's a sign of maturity and demonstrates a desire to become the best you can be. Therefore, if it seems like you're continually depressed, or know of someone who is, don't be ashamed or shy; get some professional assistance. Daily depression is called "clinical depression" and requires treatment and therapy. This depression is not caused by outside events or influences, but by inside negative and slanted perceptions and interpretations of events. Forgetting good times and dwelling on bad times, withdrawal, lack of energy, and inability to sleep are all symptoms to be aware of.

Until lately, the most common treatment for clinical depression has been anti-depressant drugs. However, a form of psychotherapy called "cognitive therapy" developed by Dr. Aaron T. Beck at the University of Pennsylvania is now used, with exciting and remarkable lasting results. Cognitive therapists state that depressed patients consistently have negative views of the world and question the evidence of a positive result. They tend to look at the worst side of everything. To combat this, when the patient says, "I'm a failure," the therapist helps him or her realize that he or she is *not* a failure by emphasizing his or her past accomplishments. He then gives the depressed person some tasks that he or she can easily and immediately succeed at doing. So if you're depressed, you can do the same! Get involved in doing something that comes easy to you. Soon you'll snap out of your depression and will be able to continue with your life. This cognitive therapy is just another documented use of the best therapy of all — positive thinking!

In conclusion, I trust you have caught the vision of this chapter and now realize the difference between causes and effects — seeds and fruits. For in this simple knowledge lies the solution to all our problems and challenges in life. When this knowledge is put into practice, alcohol, smoking, and drug abuse will decrease as it should; drunk driving will be eliminated; and because the seeds of a good self-concept will now be planted, depression will cease and suicide will become extinct. Knowing what we know now, it really can be this easy! Remember the genie inside you. Remember the unlimited power you have within you to change for the best. Now go for it!

Chapter Ten

"People Power"

How to Recondition Your Life

Have you ever wondered why you think or act as you do? Have you wondered why your family has been partial to a certain political party for several generations or wondered why they philosophize a specific way about most everything? Have you wondered why most kids set goals only as high as their parents do, play the same sports the older brothers do, and go into similar work that their fathers or mothers are in? If so, the answers to these and similar inquiries are not many, but only one. The primary reason we think and act as we do is because we've been conditioned to do so. Being right or wrong, sound or absurd, has nothing to do with it. Conditioning is different than anything we've talked about, goes deeper than positive mental attitude, and is essential to understand before you read the following chapter on goal-setting. Therefore, in preparation, "conditioning" is discussed now. Portions of this information come from an interview with the brilliant Leo Presley.

The Power of Conditioning

The conditioning process affects us throughout our lives. In fact, it begins to shape our attitudes when we are tiny children and continues to govern our outlook on life until

we die. For example, at birth, humans know only two fears — the fear of loud noises and the fear of falling. All other fears are learned. If we were to take a loaded pistol and hold it at a baby's head, the child would probably grab it, put the barrel in its mouth, and suck on it. But as the child grows older and learns to be afraid, it becomes conditioned to fear certain things. In fact, concerning the gun just mentioned, the child eventually becomes conditioned to fear that gun, whether or not it is loaded. We react to many other fears in the same way, regardless of what the true facts are.

Because this is true, conditioning is also used in the training of animals. A circus elephant is kept in its living area by only a weak chain placed around its leg and locked to a small stake driven a few inches into the ground. Why doesn't the elephant use its enormous power to break the little chain and free itself? Because it's been conditioned to believe it can't! As soon as the elephant is born, a chain is placed around its foot. When it tries to walk around, it cannot. At that time, the baby elephant is not strong enough to pull the stake out, and after several weeks, it literally quits trying. Now the elephant is defeated, tamed, and captured. No matter how much he grows, strengthens, and changes physically, the elephant remains conditioned to believe he is bound and will not change until he is reconditioned to do so.

People become conditioned in much the same way. A twelve-year-old girl went swimming with her friends. Two boys at the pool made fun of her, calling her "bow legs," drawing attention to her skinny body. A giant complex immediately captured her mind. Even though this little girl has now grown, filled out, and developed into a gorgeous eighteen-year-old, she has been conditioned to believe that her legs are ugly and bowed; she still refuses to wear shorts or a bathing suit in public. Her legs could now win every beauty contest on earth, but she has been conditioned to believe just the opposite.

Too Much Media Conditioning

Because conditioning plays such an influential part in what we do, and because the media has become aware of this power, we as TV viewers must beware. In fact, television networks, newspapers, and radio stations have so much influence it's scary! Statistics prove that most sex crimes are committed by someone who has regular access to pornographic material. And most pornography is purchased as a result of an individual's seeing something promiscuous on TV. In addition to promiscuity, the majority of TV programs also use profanity, portray businessmen as crooks and greedy evil men, and show or imply premarital and extramarital lustful sex relationships as "true love." Racial tension is provoked, class distinction is drilled in, murders and rapes are shown, and love of money is emphasized. If you think I'm exaggerating and feel TV doesn't have any effect on our subconscious minds and subsequent conscious actions, why, then, do companies spend literally billions of dollars on TV advertising? Simply because they know it truly does affect and influence us. It is the foremost conditioning tool known to man!

Children and young people watch thousands of hours of television. Starting at three years of age, the average child watches four hours of TV per day until five years of age. That's 4,368 hours — well before they even start the first grade! After five years of age, the hours per day drop substantially, but by the time the average child is eighteen he still has watched more than 13,832 hours of TV. The average twenty-five-year-old has seen 18,000 hours of television.

So how are we being conditioned? What are Americans being conditioned to think and how are they being conditioned to act? In an interesting UPI news story entitled "TV Violence Enrages Cat," the impact and influence of TV was substantiated once and for all. In the middle of a Sunday night television program, the normally mellow, lazy, quiet, slow-moving, loving pet cat of the Blood family in Nevers, France, suddenly turned into a ferocious feline and started scratching and biting members of the family. The wounds were so severe that two of the stunned family members, Mrs. Blood and her daughter-in-law, had to be taken to the hospital for treatment and anti-rabies shots.

And what was the movie being shown on TV that the cat and the family had been watching? It was a mystery film about a violent cat entitled *Cat and Mouse!*

Hey! If TV can condition a quiet cat to be a wild monster in a few minutes, what has it done to us young people over the years? Think about it!

America's young people are America's number one resource, but now they've become America's most endangered species. Something must be done! We need to change the present input of our conditioning processes and do it now. You can't plant the seed tonight and pick the fruit tomorrow. Therefore, the sooner we start, the better off we'll be.

What are the benefits of self-evaluation and reconditioning? What has already happened, and what could happen, through proper conditioning?

Our Best Resource — People

After World War II, Japan as a country was virtually destroyed. It had nothing going for it as far as economic progress, and its natural resources after the war almost didn't exist. Sure, America gave Japan money, but as far as economic resources, Japan had none. But the resource Japan did have was people.

The resource of people is by far the best and most important resource any country can have. And, as was proven by Japan, it's really the only one needed.

With absolutely no internally owned and developed business, Japan flew past America and became the world's steel industry leader in the 1950s. In the 1960s Japan surpassed America and led the world in the auto industry. Japan's goal in the 1970s was to be the world leader in the manufacture of computer/copier products. And again they climbed the achievement ladder until they now are leading the world market in that area as well. And this is because of people power! Japan's population has been conditioned to produce, conditioned to succeed, and conditioned to never quit until the task has been accomplished in a winning way.

If you could be lucky enough to travel to Japan and spend some time there, you would be amazed! They have no drug problems, very little crime, and on a typical street in the middle of the day, you would seldom see any litter. If there is any around, people actually stop and pick it up. Why? The Japanese take pride in themselves and in their country. They have been conditioned to be positive, hard-working, honest, proud, and responsible. Conditioning is the key!

Conditioning comes as a result of knowledge. And knowledge (how we perceive something to be) comes as a result of experience and environment. Because of this, each of us is who we are and acts as we do because of how we have been conditioned?

Prejudice and Conditioning

I feel the most devastating concept that Americans have been conditioned to and led to believe is human prejudice. In the past we have been taught, and I admit oftentimes without intent, that minorities are inferior. Anything in the minority is intimidated, ridiculed, supressed, and many times discarded. For example, an overweight girl in a large group of "Twiggys" is in the minority — she is made to feel inferior. And a kid with pimples in a group of smooth faces is in the minority — he, consciously or subconsciously, is made to feel inferior. Our society learns and uses the saying, "They are as different as black and white." In this statement alone, prejudice is taught and remembered as we are conditioned to believe there is a vast difference between black and white — that the two colors are at opposite ends of the spectrum. What, then, are "white" people conditioned to believe regarding "black" people? And what are "black" people conditioned to believe about "white" people?

In a social setting we automatically notice and compare color and immediately establish prejudice as we count numbers and label the minority. Then, as usual, and either consciously or subconsciously, the minority is made to feel inferior.

Recently I attended the National Speakers Association convention in Chicago along with hundreds of people from all over America and the world. While there, I became close friends with a man from Australia, and at the end of the convention we stayed an extra day to see the sights. We decided to visit the Museum of Science and Industry located on the south side of the city. When we bought our commuter train tickets, the teller looked at us quizzically, but it didn't bother us. After a fifteen-minute wait the train finally came and we boarded. Things seemed normal until the first stop when suddenly all the "white" folks except my Australian buddy and myself got off the train. More "blacks" got on. The second stop came and again more "black" people got on board. From then on, every stop put us more and more in the minority. We got deeper and deeper into the all-"black" section of Chicago, and things began to get a little hairy. I felt like a chicken in a fox house. Everyone was staring at us like we were stark naked! Then, to top it off, my Australian mate, who hadn't seen that many "black" people in his whole life (not to mention all at once) and who still thought they liked to be called Negroes, leaned over to me and, in total innocence, said in his accent, loud enough for everyone in the car to hear, "They'e sha a lot of nigras ont thea. Maybe we'e on the wrong train?"

Now what does what he called them sound like to you? Everyone on our entire car heard him and now really started to "eye the tiger"!

The train finally stopped at Fifty-Sixth South — our stop — and we got off just in time to miss catching the bus for the last fifteen-minute ride to the museum. There we were, stranded in an all "black" neighborhood, standing out like encyclopedia salesmen on a street corner, trying to be cool and act "bad," when in reality we were nervous as cats outside a dog pound.

Car after car slowed down as they passed by, their occupants staring at us in total amazement. And again, there we were, very alone, very scared, and thinking up appropriate words to have engraved on our tombstones.

We were on the street corner a total of three minutes when my "Aussie" companion made another observation. "Hey, mite, you think we'd betta go bock in git the 'ell out ev hea?" I thought for a total time of about two-tenths of a second and replied, "You bet! Let's go!" So we strolled back across the street, back down the steps, back past all the dudes standing around wondering what the "flip" we were doing, and waited fifteen minutes for the next train to come. Finally it came, we made it back downtown, and got off the train. As soon as we were safe again, my buddy's face lit up like a Christmas tree in total relief and joy. We caught a cab and went to our hotel.

Both a taxi driver and a policeman parked outside the hotel told us that it was a miracle we got out of that part of town without being robbed, mugged, or worse. They explained that the only thing that saved us was that the residents of that neighborhood must have thought we were a bit cuckoo and totally crazy, or undercover policemen.

Why did I go into such length and detailed description with this experience? Why did I call people "black" and "white" when I previously stated that we should not distinguish between the two? I did it to vividly explain the conditioning process that has gone on for centuries in the black and white cultures of America. We have racial boundaries, unwritten no-trespassing laws, and hostile feelings for each other, and we don't even know why! And for those who think they do know why, most reasons are because of something that happened to them or to a family member many years ago. The prejudice might even have been passed down through several generations. This sense-less hate comes not from what actually happened, but from the conditioning process. Hey! This is ridiculous! We need to forgive and forget! And, yes, it is as simple as that!

This experience in Chicago taught me several things, one of which is how it really feels to be a "minority." Let me tell you — no one, of any race, color, or creed, should ever be made to feel as I felt! It's wrong that people should make fellow human beings (total strangers who have done nothing to them) feel inferior, intimidated, and unequal because of their birthright, ancestry, or beliefs. I realize white people (the majority) have been making non-white people feel like this for decades. And merely passing civil rights laws and writing them in books is not going to change people's thinking and behavior. We need to recondition our society to change its ways. Black people are *not* inferior! White people are *not* inferior! Indians are *not* inferior! No one is! Mexican-Americans, Japanese-Americans, and all other "kinds" of Americans are just

169

that — Americans! People of all races, colors, and creeds fought and died to gain and preserve this freedom; therefore, people of all races, colors, and creeds are entitled to total and equal benefits of this freedom. We need to accept this fact and not make race and skin color an issue. A person does not have to say, "One of my best friends is a black man," or "I'm not prejudiced, I work with a white guy." They're only people! Why differentiate between skin color and people?

Books, Balloons, and Ice Cream

Don't judge a book or anything else by its *color*. And it's not what's on the outside of the helium balloon that makes it rise, it's what's *inside* that makes it go up. We were not born in the same place, with the same talents, or brought up the same way. Obviously we don't have the same size noses, ears, teeth, height, weight, or the same color of hair. Why, then, should color of skin make any difference?

In order to change this human prejudice we've grown accustomed to, we need to recondition our thinking by changing our perception. Think of mankind as ice cream. There are many flavors and colors of ice cream. But regardless of whether it's chocolate, vanilla, strawberry, or any other flavor, it's still ice cream and must be treated and handled in the exact same, delicate way. All ice cream is made out of the same basic ingredients — only small recipe changes alter the flavoring and color. And regardless of color and flavor, all ice cream will melt when heated and will freeze when chilled.

People are exactly the same way. They are people — nothing more and especially nothing less! It would be an ugly and boring world if everyone was the same color and looked and acted alike. But, as in the case of ice cream, when we finally take all these flavors of people and treat them alike, the world will suddenly become happy, caring, and peaceful.

If this is ever going to happen, we must not wait for others to change. We, the youth of America, must lead the way and begin today! We must simply accept people for who and what they are and always look for the good in others.

What Do You Look For?

Several decades ago Japan was walled in as a nation. During that period, nature was extensively studied by small groups of Japanese people as a way of learning lessons of life.

One day, when a teacher was leaving the city to study nature, he was stopped by three men. One asked the teacher to bring him a rose so that he might study the petals. The second man requested a hawthorn twig. The third asked him for a lily so that he might remember the lesson of purity.

That night the teacher returned to the city and delivered the requested parcels to the three men. Suddenly the man with the rose said, "Here's a thorn on the stem." The second man said, "My hawthorn twig has a dead leaf dangling from it." And the third man, encouraged by this fault-finding, said, "There is dirt clinging to the roots of my lily."

At this, the teacher took back the gifts from the three men and in return gave the thorn to the man who had the rose. To the man who had the hawthorn twig, he gave the dead leaf. And to the one who had the beautiful lily, he gave the dirt. Keeping the three gifts from nature for himself, the teacher explained, "Each of you now has what attracted you first. And you got what you were looking for — the first thing you saw. Each of you gets to keep what caught your attention, and I will keep the magnificent rose, the strong hawthorn twig, and the pure white lily for the beauty I see in them."

Look for only the beauty and the good in others. Recondition your thinking and behavior, and together we will recondition the thinking and behavior of the world. Everyone was born to succeed, but it sure will be lonesome if you're the only one who actually does succeed. Therefore, you must help others! Success must be shared! I admonish all of us to live by, practice, and breathe Zig Ziglar's famous words, "You can get everything in life you want, if you help enough other people get what they want!" Keep this in mind as you proceed to the next chapter on goal-setting, which will teach you how to make this chapter, this book, and Zig's words come true for you.

Chapter Eleven

"Where Am I Going?"

How to Set Goals and Become Well-Rounded

As we begin this chapter, I want to remind you of your fantastic imaginative powers. I want you to use your imagination and think of something great — something so exciting in life that you would give anything to be able to accomplish it. Don't hold back. I want you to go for it!

George Bernard Shaw put it better than I when he said, "You see things as they are and say, Why? But I dream of things that never were and say, Why not?"

This is what I want you to do. Dream some impossible dreams. Reach for unreachable stars. You've got to aim high — remember this song: "On top of Old Smoky all covered with snow, I lost my best bird dog by aiming too low." Set your sights high and remember, you are limitless because you have imagination, so use it.

Now that you've had time to think about this, I promise you that you can make your dreams come true. How you do it is what this chapter is all about.

Dr. William James, a renowned psychologist, stated that even the most outstanding, effective humans, the greatest minds of our time, utilize only about 9 or 10 percent of their total mental potential. Most people utilize only about 1 or 2 percent of their mental potential. Why is this? Why can't we ever seem to reach our potential? How and when are we

If You Don't Know Where You Are Going

How Are You Going to Know When You Get There?

going to overcome this mental resistance and these self-inflicted barriers that are holding us back? Remember, every living human has an infinite capability to become greater. Why, then, don't we?

The answer is, we don't set goals. Sure, we have dreams, but we need clearly defined goals!

Dreams imply thinking and wandering, while goals signify specific action and doing. Goals are the tools used to make our dreams come true.

If the value of setting goals is still vague, this true story should solve that.

The story takes place in 1957. Outside Kiezar Stadium in San Francisco, California, a tall, skinny, ten-year-old boy shuffled about, waiting to get inside the stadium.

He was raised in the North Beach Ghettos of the San Francisco area and had no money to buy a ticket. Therefore, he had to wait until the end of the third quarter, when the gate guard left, to sneak in. Sneaking in wasn't as easy for him as it would have been for other young boys because he had trouble walking. You see, malnutrition had taken its toll and he had suffered from a vitamin D deficiency. Rickets had left his legs weak and bowed and he had to walk with the aid of steel splints.

Slowly but surely he made his way into the stadium and positioned himself right in the middle of the players' entrance tunnel. There he patiently waited for the game to end so he could make his dream come true. He had waited all year for this football game and now it had finally come. The San Francisco 49ers and the Cleveland Browns were playing, and this would be his big chance to see, and hopefully meet, his idol, Jim Brown. Jim Brown was the Cleveland Brown's all -pro running back who held every rushing record in the NFL.

As the final gun went off, this young, wiry lad struggled to stand tall so he wouldn't miss his dream moment. Finally, it came! Jim Brown turned the corner and walked toward him. As he passed by, the lad held out a piece of paper, asking politely for his autograph. Brown graciously signed it and turned for the locker room. But before he could get away, the little boy tugged on the back of Brown's jersey, stopping him once again. Brown turned to see who it was and was met with the proud confession, "Mr. Brown, I have your picture on my wall. My family can't afford a TV but I watch you on the neighbor's set every time I get a chance. I know what your records are and all about everything you do. You're the greatest! You're my idol!"

Jimmy Brown, beaming a smile, put his hand on the boy's shoulder. "Thanks," he said, and turned again toward the locker room. But the little boy still wasn't down! He reached up and tugged on Brown's jersey a second time, turning him around again. Knowing who it was this time, Jim looked down to find those same big, brown eyes looking up at him just as before. "Yes," Jim asked. The boy cleared his throat, held his shoulders back and his head high, and matter-of-factly said, "Mr. Brown, do you know what? One day I'm going to break every record you hold!"

Brown was so taken aback by this statement that he had to ask, "What is your name, son?"

The boy replied, "Orenthal James. My friends call me O.J."

The young boy quickly grew, and within a few short years O. J. Simpson earned a scholarship and became the Heisman Trophy winner at the University of Southern California. He then became the NFL's number one college draft pick and, despite the fact that he played on two of the worst teams in pro football, O. J. became the greatest running back in NFL history, breaking all but three of Jim Brown's records, just as he said he would. And he certainly would have broken those last three records if he hadn't suffered knee injuries which required surgery and cut his career short.

What an awesome story! An intense ten-year-old boy who came from that kind of adversity, actually knew what he wanted, set his sights high, and accomplished his goals. He, in fact, proved that this goal-setting stuff really works.

And now Simpson still continues to dream, set, and reach goals, and succeed. As you know, O. J. doesn't run through airports anymore — he flies!

Just as O. J. had a dream, set a goal, and worked hard to accomplish it, so can we. You don't have to be a crippled kid or a professional athlete to make this goal-setting stuff work — anyone in anything can do it!

Because goal-setting is the key to accomplishment, let's define *goals* more clearly: "The mark set as the limit to a race; aim or purpose; an area or object toward which play is directed in order to score." How do goals affect us in our everyday lives? The answer is: in a big way. You see, every day, everyone needs to know whether he has won or lost. This is where goals come into play. The only way we have to keep score is to set goals. They tell us when we finish the task, score, or cross the line.

The other night I was speaking at a father-and-son night at an elementary school. They asked me to speak on personal motivation and goal-setting. I decided that I would demonstrate my point and took a basketball with me as my visual aid. The setting was a large cafeteria with no basketball facilities or sports equipment in sight — the perfect environment to try out my plan. After talking to the group for a brief minute, I asked for a volunteer to help me. I picked one eager boy and had him come up in front of the room. I threw him the basketball and told him to make a basket. He dribbled around, put a few moves on, looked up to shoot, and then stopped. A puzzled look came over his face, and I asked him why he had stopped. He answered simply, "There's no basket." I needled him on and told him to shoot it anyway. In total amazement the kid threw the ball up against the wall. "Did you make it?" I asked. The kid gave a classic answer. "How am I supposed to know if I made it? There was no hoop to shoot for."

As the boy took his seat, he looked at me like I was nuts and muttered, "What an idiot!"

My demonstration had worked! I then drew the conclusion. Life, if you think about it, is exactly the same way. If we go through life without goals, we'll spend all of our time running up and down the field and never scoring. We need to have visual goals; things we can actually picture and see. We need to have baskets to put the ball through, goal lines to work toward, targets to shoot for. Without them, we don't have direction in life and we won't know where we're going. And if we don't know where we're going, we won't know when we get there. It's like the conversation I heard between a little girl and a neighbor from her street. "Hello, missy! Want a ride?" "No, thanks. I'm walking back from one now!"

176

Goals are essential for life. Goals are the vehicle by which we turn our fantasies into reality and our hopes into history. Goals give us a specific purpose to life; they give us direction and reason to live. Dr. Dennis Waitley summed it up when he said, "Goals keep us going when things go wrong and keep us growing when things are right." Goals to us are like the stars at night to the sailor at sea — we chart our course by them. A goal is a compass that points the way.

Why We Should Set Goals

I talk a lot about believing in yourself, believing that you can do something. Well, goal-setting is the natural result, the next step beyond believing you can do it. Therefore the first reason we should set goals is that it puts our thoughts, beliefs, and dreams into action.

Earl Nightingale once asked the question, "Have you ever wondered why so many work so hard and honestly without ever achieving anything in particular? And others don't seem to work hard, and yet they seem to have everything? They seem to have the magic touch." He answered himself: "It is because of goals. . . . some have them and some don't. People will succeed because they know where they are going. A person who is thinking about a worthwhile goal is going to reach it, because that is what he is thinking about, and we do what we think about doing." Success comes as a direct result of believing you can do something and then setting goals to do it. Remember that the greater your belief is, the more rapid your progress will be. Didn't someone wise once say, "As a man thinketh, so is he."

Another reason we should want to set goals is that goal-setting helps organize our lives so that we can accomplish more. If we are ever going to learn how to maximize our brain capacity, we must get organized and achieve order. Order creates space. For example, if you organize and systematically arrange a closet or a drawer, you create space. The mind is exactly the same way. If you organize your mind, you create space and allow for more things to be put into it. It is also easier, then, to get things out of it because your mind is now a library instead of a depository.

To be organized also implies something else. If we place things we need to get done in a time block, decide when and where they must be accomplished, and then simply concentrate on the "now," we will be organized and become successful in every phase of life.

> There may be nothing wrong with you,
> The way you live, the work you do,
> But I can very plainly see
> Exactly what is wrong with me.
> It isn't that I'm indolent
> Or dodging duty by intent,
> I work as hard as anyone,
> And yet I get so little done.
> The morning goes, the noon is here,
> Before I know, the night is near.
> And all around me, I regret
> Are things I haven't finished yet.
> "If I could just get organized,"
> I oftentimes have realized.
> Not all that matters is the man,
> The man must also have a plan.
> With you, there may be nothing wrong,
> But here's my trouble right along —
> I do the things that don't amount
> To very much of no account,
> That really seem important, though,
> And let a lot of matters go.
> I nibble this, I nibble that,
> But never finish what I'm at.
> I work as hard as anyone,
> And yet I get so little done.
> I'd do so much, you'd be surprised,
> If I could just get organized.

Author Unknown

A third reason we should want to set goals is that no one ever accomplishes anything of consequence without first setting a goal. Each of us is born to succeed and shape a destiny for ourselves. And the extent of that destiny is measured by the personal goals we set. Therefore, goal-setting is the strongest human force for motivation. Not fear motivation, which comes from threat ("I'll get a gun"); not reward or incentive motivation ("Pay me more money, I'll give you a prize"); but self-motivation ("I want to do it"), which is the best kind of motivation.

Self-Motivation

Personal goals, coupled with a strong sense of purpose, give us the ability to make wise decisions. What it boils down to is that goal-setting helps us make up our minds.

After *we* (meaning not someone else) make up our minds and decide the direction *we* want to go, the action part comes easy. It comes as a result of this self-motivation. If we want to do it for ourselves, if we're striving to accomplish the goal that *we* want to do, it will get done! The key, then, is that we must set our own goals and decide on our own timetable. No one else can do this for us.

Because self-motivation is the most important single ingredient in successful goal-setting, we need to learn how to develop it. To cultivate self-motivation and make it a constant, natural part of your life, you, the goal-setter, must satisfactorily answer three questions: "Why should I?" "What's in it for me?" "Will it make me feel wanted and important?" If you can honestly answer these questions, self-motivation will definitely be present. And as I mentioned, this in turn almost guarantees your success in accomplishing the task at hand. Remember, when *you* want to do the task, the task gets done!

The final reason we should set goals is that goal-setting is powerful! It constantly reminds us of where we're going and what we want to do. Goals help us see ourselves as we are, where we are. They help us learn from the past and project for the future. They help us implement our thoughts and dreams and provide a way for us to evaluate our progress and situation so we can change, if we need to, to stay on course.

In other words, the road to success and personal perfection is simple and straight if we set some realistic, well-thought-out, documented, predetermined goals.

As you begin to set your goals, be aware that life consists of many areas where you need to improve yourself. You will tend to reach for perfection only in areas that interest you or that come easy to you. But don't cheat yourself! You don't know all the areas that interest you until you've tried them. Therefore, set goals in all areas and remember — the ultimate goal is to become well-rounded and the best you can possibly be.

The six areas I'm referring to are: physical, mental, spiritual, financial, social, and family. All are important. All are necessary if we are to become all that we were meant to be.

A Human "Stereo"

Picture for a moment a sophisticated stereo system and how it works. It has six speakers: a treble speaker, a bass speaker, a speaker for the percussion, one for the lead vocal, one for the harmonies, and one for the extremely high sounds. In order to get the best sound from a record being played on this stereo, all the speakers have to be plugged in. If one comes unplugged, the sound becomes distorted. Imagine how distorted the music would sound if two or three speakers were unplugged. We would hear only high treble, no bass or percussion, and goofy-sounding vocals.

On the other hand, if we are to hear the best possible sound, and hear the recorded music the way its creator wanted us to hear it — we need to have all stereo speakers working at maximum efficiency.

Human beings are exactly the same way. Each of us was also created in stereo. Each of us is a highly technical stereo system using several speakers to project our talents or sounds. They, too, need to be constantly serviced and tuned. They, too, need to all be plugged in and working at the same time if we are going to be who we are meant to be — if we are going to be the best we can be.

Let's quickly examine these speakers of life — these six areas or sides of life which make up the well-rounded individual.

Physical

The first goal or speaker we must tune up is the physical one. The dictionary defines *physical* as "material as opposed to mental or spiritual; bodily, relating to the body."

I bet you've heard someone ask you today, "How are you? And you probably answered without thinking about it, "I'm fine, thank you. How are you?" But I mean, how are you *really?* How is your body? Are you well-proportioned and trim or are you overweight and roly-poly? Are you puffing after climbing a flight of stairs? Do your muscles ache the day after you exercise? How about your insides? When you sneeze or cough, do you blow smoke rings? Is your blood flowing with dragster gas from sipping too much brew? Do you see funny, blurry, slow-motion movements all day long because of too much "maui yowie"? You need to evaluate these things.

You see, our bodies are finely-tuned thoroughbreds, ready for the track. Why, then, do so many people abuse them? Would you give a million-dollar racehorse cigarettes, alcohol, drugs, and bad food? I know if you were a professional jockey and your life and living depended on how well your racehorse performed, you would take great care of it. Well, your body is your horse and it's the only transportation you'll ever have! Isn't it worthy to be babied and cared for, too?

We are what we feel, and we feel according to what goes into our bodies. If we take care of our bodies, we'll feel good. We'll feel like doing more and therefore we'll do more. Every phase and area of life will be enhanced and will become better as we tune up our physical speaker and bring our fitness up to par.

Mental

Let's plug in the second speaker of life — the mental one. Webster defines *mental* to mean, "of or relating to the mind. That which is thought. The capacity and functioning of the brain."

We've extensively discussed the limitless potential and amazing capacity our brains have, so let's move on and mention some important points that may be used to better the mental area of life. To begin with, if we're going to better utilize our brain capacity, we need to engage in continual education and develop the ability to listen. These two habits must come first and be an on-going thing before we can effectively tune up our mental speaker. To assist you in your continual education, put good magazines and books in strategic places, such as the bathroom, bedrooms, and kitchen. Listen to motivational and educational tapes while you're driving or riding in the car.

181

Next, we need to remember that everything in life that we accomplish, and every goal that has ever been set, started in our minds. Our minds control our bodies and our lives. We're only as big as our minds let us be. Therefore, don't put a damper on yourself. Don't hold back. Master your mind and go for it! Reach for the stars — you have potential to get there!

Spiritual

This brings us to the third speaker — the spiritual or emotional area of life.

Webster defines *spiritual* as "relating to or consisting of spirit; relating to sacred matters, and morals."

For some reason, whenever the word *spiritual* is mentioned, we tend to cringe and think, "Don't preach to me; don't talk about religion; back off!" Well, you can relax. We're not going to discuss religion or God, even though maybe we should. There is much more to the spiritual side than religion, and this is what we are going to discuss.

According to the Thomas Jefferson Research Center, when America won its independence, the spiritual side of life accounted for over 90 percent of the content of the school books. By 1926, the figure was only 6 percent, and today it is virtually zero. Why has there been this decline in the awareness of the spiritual side of life and the importance of teaching morals? The spiritual area is just as important to being well-rounded today as it was two hundred years ago. In fact, if we look around ourselves at the problems in the world, the teaching of moral and spiritual values may be even more important now than it ever was!

Concerning morality, Peter A. French said, "Morality's primary function is to constrain people from doing those things that have a deteriorative effect on the biological, sociological, and economic human condition." In other words, morality helps us maintain a minimum standard of decency by discouraging us from doing things that have a bad effect on self and society.

Morality is the regulator — the watchman — the reference point — the determining factor of the outcome of our standard of decency. It can be categorized into two areas: Our moral judgments advocate either (1) the preservation of, or (2) the deterioration of, society and self. Therefore, everything we think, hear, do, see, or say fits into one or the other. Our moral views have either a positive or a negative effect on all our events.

In discussing this "morality" in terms of education, questions always arise: "What is the standard of decency? What is the satisfactory, fundamental, adequate model of this ideal 'moral' human condition? What specific moral code should we teach and follow?" The only two choices follow.

The first, the "new morality," promotes open lust and sex because pornography is amusing and harmless; marriage is no big deal; tell the truth only when it benefits you; more pay for less work; don't seek a job because unemployment is paying a check to me every month; sell drugs to make a quick buck; get bombed on alcohol; let tomorrow take care of itself.

The second, the "established, traditional morality," supports marriage and a family unit that is the foundation of success; strong families equal a strong community and nation; sex is not dirty but sacred (you may create a baby — think about how important that task is and how important that makes you); honesty is always the best policy; pay equals productivity; getting drunk and taking drugs are reasonless; goals should be good, clean, powerful, and positive.

With this brief overview of some of the characteristics of our two "moral choices," you be the judge! Ponder these ideals and decide on the best moral code to live by. I didn't say to choose the easiest code or the most popular code. Just use your conscience and your common sense, and decide which standard of living is the best in terms of everyone's interest — which code of ethics will reap the best results in stabilizing society in the long run.

And as you decide, keep in mind the causes of why the great empires like Rome and Greece fell. Historically, nineteen out of the last twenty-one countries that have fallen have collapsed from within, and not from outside forces! These disasters have all been related to the spiritual side and moral values. You see, the evil things that are happening around us happen in direct proportion to the amount of time we spend teaching morality in our homes and schools. I realize that some parents and schools do teach moral values, but in so doing, these discussions cannot be conducted in a moral vacuum where every choice is presented as if it was equal to every other available choice. Such an approach would imply that there is no particular value in any value, and it would obscure the very kind of knowledge the students need in order to make responsible value judgments. This method of teaching may be acceptable for other subjects, but it doesn't "cut it" in teaching morality. Young people need direction in this matter and cannot be left to explore the other options as is usually done in education. And this is *not* propaganda — this is intelligent, sound, historically proven, necessary education!

As we learn about morality, we need to also realize that morality involves honesty, integrity, justice, responsibility, and commitment to a cause. It means doing unto others as you would have them do unto you. It has to do with being a good person, being a good neighbor, and being a just and honest friend. Even if we had no holy books that preached morality, even if there were never prophets or "Sons" who taught "love thy neighbor," or even if you are atheist, it still would be much better to do what is right, to speak the truth, to go the second mile, and to forgive our enemies and serve our fellowmen than it would be to live any other way.

I feel strongly about the importance of tuning up this inner-self, spiritual, emotional, moral speaker because, to me, the spiritual side of life is the most important side of life. It encompasses much more than philosophy and answering the questions, Where did I come from? Why am I here? and Where am I going? Tuning up your spiritual understanding is the key to successful living.

Financial

The fourth speaker is the financial one. This involves the moneymaking area of our existence. Webster defines *financial* as "having to do with finance or financiers.

Dealing with money matters. To raise or provide funds for, to sell or supply."

As you well know, we all have to have at least a little bit of money to survive in our society. We have no choice. Money is the trading object the world has adopted to purchase goods and services. Therefore, we have a need for a financial side of life. And it is as important as the other sides. Our temporal existence depends upon it.

Have you ever asked yourself, "What do I want out of life and how much does it cost?" If not, it's worth looking into!

Many may disagree with me that money is important and necessary and may misquote the Bible saying, "Money is the root of all evil." But this is not the quote. This famous phrase says, "The *love* of money is the root of all evil." Money is not bad. Making money is not evil, assuming it has been honestly earned. We must support ourselves, and making money is how we do it. We need not apologize for making a profit. It's important to our survival, and the more we make, the better off we'll be! Money comes as we render service, and as we render more service we make more money. If we work harder and smarter than others, we deserve to have more things. And the extra money can be put in a savings account, invested in an interest-drawing deal to earn more money, used to buy the "hottest" car on campus, or put into college, clothes, dating, parties, skiing, or recreation. Or better still, if we make more than we need, we can help others by giving to charities such as the National Multiple Sclerosis Society, or maybe we can even provide a Christmas for a needy family.

Financial goals are important. They affect the lives of many more than just you or your family. For example, when your dad or mother's business grows and expands through their hard work and dedicated service, sure, they make more profit. But a company has to make a profit in order to stay in business. More money provides more jobs and better pay, which in turn creates more money and a better standard of living for those who work for their company. This in turn provides more tax dollars which build schools and pay teachers who teach us so we can one day continue this cycle. If your parents work for someone else, this principle also holds true. As they work harder and produce more business, they get raises, and the company grows, which creates more jobs.

Do you want to be financially secure when you're older? If you do, in order for you to get there, you must start now! Get into the habit of saving, experience the rewards of hard work, and learn the value of a dollar while you're young. Remember, you can have anything you want in this world if you're willing to earn it and pay the price to get it.

Accomplishing your financial goals is important, for it allows you the time and money to join a spa and work on your physical side; the leisure time to enjoy your family side; the study time to develop your mental side; the reflection time to pursue your spiritual side; and plenty of time for play in your social side.

Social

Webster defines *social* as "one who is marked by pleasant companionship with one's friends. Of or relating to human society. The interaction of the group and its members."

Participating in the social side of life is a very important part of being the best we can be. It's the area of life that helps us become well-rounded. It's the part of life where we learn from others and share ourselves with our friends. Tuning up this speaker is important because each one of us, whether we're introverted or extroverted, needs to learn how to communicate. And tuning up the social speaker not only teaches us how to communicate, it also provides an atmosphere and opportunity wherein we *can* communicate. It's in the social setting where we develop relationships and friendships that help us meet our three basic needs: love, importance, and security. As we fulfill these needs, we become happy and content and motivated to do better than ever before. The natural overflow effect resulting from this contentment will positively influence each of our other areas of life and insure our eventual success and happiness.

In conclusion, I leave you one last bit of social wisdom: when you are at home, watch your temper; when you are in the company of others, watch your tongue; and when you are alone, watch your thoughts.

Family

The last of the six speakers of life that we need to tune up and develop is the family speaker — the side of life that takes place at home. Webster defines *family* to mean, "a group of persons with common ancestry, composed of parents and their children, living under one roof under one head-of-household."

Obviously, as children grow older and move out, or if a divorce takes place and the family is split, this definition does not hold true. But generally speaking, for our teenage years, I feel the rest of my comments apply to all of us.

There are many views of what a family is, but I believe a family is a group of friends with the same father and mother. And these friends know you as you are, understand who you've been, accept who you've become, and still gently invite you to grow. These friends are not ordinary friends, they're special friends. They're the friends who are the first to come in when the whole world has gone out. They love you for who you are and not for what you look like. They know you're unique, and they won't compare you with others, especially other members of the family. They're friends you can talk to in confidence about anything. They're people you can expect help, guidance, and concern from during a crisis. These friends love you just because you're you.

The family is the fundamental foundation of any society and therefore, if our communities and nation are to become better and stronger, we must have good, strong families.

As I've mentioned my feelings about families, perhaps some of you started evaluating your own situations. Perhaps you started thinking and realized your family is not as good and strong and closely knit as it should or could be.

If this is the case, don't get discouraged, just change it! Call your family together, or maybe just your mom and dad alone, express your concerns, and make your suggestions. Set some goals, both as individuals and as a group. Then decide together how you can change your family to make it better.

Because of the extreme and urgent importance of tuning up this area of life, I feel some suggestions could include:

187

1. (Girls) Always remember to treat your father and your brothers as you would good friends. Negotiate, compromise, and plan out your ideas, desires, and differences together. Don't take your dad and brothers and all they do for you for granted. Be just as nice, polite, and considerate to them as you would be to your boyfriend and his family.

2. (Boys) Treat your mother and your sisters the same way you treat your girlfriend or her mom. Try to impress and do sweet things for your mom the same way and to the same degree you charm and baby your girlfriend and her mom. Remember, your mother and sisters are more important than any other women on earth. Treat them like queens. Do little things and buy surprises for them like you do for other women. They should be your best female friends.

3. (Boys and Girls) Play an active role in your family. Do what you can to help around the house and in the yard. If you've never worked around the house before, then do it cautiously — I don't want anyone's parents dying of a heart attack! When the family does something together, pitch in and do it with them. Don't think you're too cool to be seen with your mother or to spend a weekend or date night with your family. This demonstrates your own self-confidence and maturity.

4. (Boys and Girls) Remember, you get out of life what you put into it, and this holds true in a family. You get out of your family what you put into it.

Decide today to make your family the greatest, most ideal family in the world. It can be if you want it to be. It can be if each family member wants it to be. And it's *never* too late! Become best friends with your mom and dad, brothers and sisters. Do things with them and for them. Your house really can become a home!

How to Set Goals

This brings us to the final section on goal-setting. How do we set goals? How do we make them work in our everyday lives?

To begin with, we need to remember that it doesn't do us

a bit of good to set a goal if we don't plan to accomplish it. We must realize that it takes determination and perserverance, intestinal fortitude and commitment to the end if we are going to make our dreams come true. This is how we make goal-setting work in our everyday lives. If we want to accomplish our goals, what we need to do is commit to accomplishing them before we get started. With this commitment, we will be able to overcome any obstacles along the way and achieve the desired results. You see, commitment causes us to be consistent, and consistency is one vital key to success. Remember this tongue-twister: "Proper, prior planning prevents poor performance."

If you learn and practice the following simple guidelines for long- and short-range goal-setting, you will effectively set goals and be consistent about achieving them. The result will be better days, months, and years for you.

Long-Range "Big" Goals

The first step in goal-setting is to think *big*. You should set your goals high. If your goals are set high, even if you don't quite reach them, your level of accomplishment will still be much higher than it would be if you merely set low, easily-attainable goals. Remember the old saying, "It's better to shoot for the stars and miss, than it is to aim for a pile of manure and hit." Don't worry about failing a few times. Occasional failure is important. The idea is not to never fail, but to always make it a surprise and not a bad habit. If you don't fail sometimes, it means you are not pushing yourself hard enough; your goals are not high enough.

It's been said, "The quality of the imagination is to flow and not to freeze." You need to keep this in mind as you choose a distant goal. And if you do, this long-range goal will help you overcome short-range frustrations.

Write Goals Down

After you set this long-range goal, or any type of goal, write it down. "A goal is only a wish until it's written down." Then let it become an obsession with you. Write it on a wallet-size card that you can always carry with you. Put it on something else big enough to hang on the wall so you won't miss it as you walk by. Your goal may be a car, some clothes, a motorcycle, an award, or a trophy. It may be college, a certain job, weight loss, or being president of a club. Whatever it is, find a picture or a printed phrase of it and always keep it somewhere in front of you. Remember, obsession is the key! Keep the goal always in your thoughts and actions. Never stop thinking about it until you've accomplished it.

Goals Create Competition

The next step is for you to concentrate on this big goal you have set and make *it* the competition. Do you remember from the other chapters that you shouldn't compete against others until you first compete against yourself? Well, this is where it pays off. A person is only as good as his competition, and therefore, if the long-range goal is big enough, it will tax your abilities and help you push yourself to your limits.

The goal must not be out of sight, but just out of reach. It has to be big enough to keep you excited, but far enough away that it stretches you to do better than you normally would. The major reason many people do not reach their goals is that the time limit that they set for accomplishing their goals is unrealistic. This is especially true with goals such as weight loss, weight gain, and body-building.

Identifying and Overcoming Obstacles

As you progress toward your goals, you will most certainly meet obstacles. But that's great! Obstacles are an important part of life. Remember that obstacles are only of the moment. If you really want to achieve your goal, you have to be able to overcome any obstacle that comes in your way, and this is easy if you just keep your eye on your goal. After you identify the obstacle, don't look *at* it; look *through* it and keep your eye on where you want to eventually be.

One of my close friends, Todd Peterson, is one degree short of Shodon in Shotokan Karate. He has given karate demonstrations in Europe, California, and Utah. One day a few years ago, he was putting on a demonstration in Dublin, Ireland. He had not been to a karate workout in over a year because of his time commitment to his business, but he consented to demonstrate his skills anyway. The group of men in attendance asked him to break two boards at the same time. Todd produced two one-inch by twelve-inch pieces of pine which he proceeded to stack together and properly position in my straightened arms. Just before he attempted to break the boards, he leaned over and whispered that he had never tried this before. He had never broken more than one board at a time, ever!

I was holding the boards for him and could see the determined look on his face as he measured the distance between himself and the boards.

Seconds later, POW! He hit those boards so hard that the force nearly knocked me down. After I caught myself and realized what had happened, I noticed the two boards were still intact. He had not broken either one of them! The crowd giggled a little bit as he stood there, embarrassed and amazed. I then noticed that the index knuckle on his right hand was cut open, bleeding badly, turning purple, and starting to swell. I figured the demonstration was over — no way could he hit the boards again with his hurting hand. But he did!

Ending the demonstration wouldn't have been a big deal, but in karate, once you challenge an obstacle or an opponent (in this case it was the two boards), you cannot back down or quit until you have defeated the opponent. Todd had explained this principle before he started.

So Todd dropped down once again into his stance, concentrated, and POW! My arms shook! The boards nearly flew from my grip, but both remained in one piece. The only thing Todd broke this time was the skin on another knuckle. Now two knuckles were badly bruised and bleeding, but Todd still refused to quit.

Being the type of exceptional individual he is, Todd was committed to overcoming the obstacle and reaching his goal, regardless of how many times it took him to do it. As he addressed the boards the third time, I could see the pained look of determination all over his face as he stared and concentrated on hitting them again. He once again dropped into his stance, took a deep breath, and POW! This time he broke both boards!

After the people left, I asked Todd to explain the breaking technique. He answered very simply and taught me not only a great lesson in enduring to the end, but also a valuable lesson about overcoming obstacles in goal-setting. Todd told me the way you break boards is to look and hit through them as if they weren't even there. The reason he couldn't break the boards the first two times was because he was looking *at* the boards instead of *through* them. He had his eye on the obstacle rather than on the goal, and until he changed his focal point, he wasn't able to break through the obstacle and accomplish his goal.

Goal-setting is the same way. If we lose sight of our goal, we'll get caught up in the frustration of obstacles along the way, detour from the path, and never achieve what we want to.

Short-Range Goals

The other type of goal other than long-range is the short-range goal, and everything we've already talked about also applies to them. When organized, these short-range goals form the step-by-step "ladder" that takes you from where you are now to where you want to be.

If you expect to accomplish a long-range goal, you must realize it doesn't happen overnight. It is a step-by-step, short-range-goal-by-short-range-goal climb to the top. You must constantly work toward your objectives every day, every hour, every second.

Detailed and Measurable Goals

As you set your goals and break them down into more specifically-defined steps, if you're doing it correctly, you will find that your list of goals will have a long-range goal on top and then will pyramid into six-month goals, monthly goals, weekly goals, daily goals, and finally, hourly goals. The hourly goals should then be placed in order of priority: Priority As, Priority Bs, and Priority Cs, Priority As being most urgent and important. Remember, the art of goal-setting is to focus on only one specific objective at a time and do it now, for there is no other priority except what needs to be done now! And make goals measurable, as they are in football — first down and ten yards to go, or third and three. This helps you break down the goals even more specifically as you go.

Specific Time Limits

Both long-range and short-range goals must have a specific time limit and a finish date attached to them. Even the time of day is important to set and write down when setting daily and hourly goals. Write: "I will accomplish my goal by such and such a time and date." Break down every goal to this point.

Delegation

Learn to delegate. Solicit the aid of other people, even specialists, to help you accomplish your goals. Remember, a problem shared is a problem halved and eventually solved. Humble yourself and realize you can't always do everything on your own. Don't be embarrassed or intimidated to ask for help for anything.

Checkpoints

Have checkpoints to determine your progress. When you purchase a car, the owner's manual always states specific times to bring your car in for service checks. This principle also holds true in goal-setting.

You need to have a series of specific checkpoint deadlines to help you meet your goals such as: "I will be finished with this short-range step by next Monday." "This goal will be met by June 1." These are great motivators as they not only allow you to look back and see how far you've come, but also allow you to look ahead to see if you're still on schedule to accomplish your goal. If you've fallen behind, these checkpoints help you decide what steps you must take to make up for lost ground.

Checkpoints also allow you to evaluate and reevaluate your goals. Keith Degreen said, "Goals should be written on paper, not chiseled in stone." Remember this as you grow, for sometimes priorities change and other exciting opportunities present themselves that will influence you to adjust your long-range goals. There is nothing wrong with this, but be cautious and take your time in making a rational, well-thought-out decision before you change direction. Give your goal every possible chance to mature and be accomplished before you set another one.

For your convenient reference, the following is a concise, numbered list of the eight goal-setting steps covered:

1. Think big. Set an exciting long-range goal. Make it your competition.

2. Write down all your goals, both long- and short-range. Keep them always in front you.

3. Identify the obstacles you must overcome and commit yourself to overcoming them.

4. Set a number of short-range goals, listing the things you have to do and the order in which you have to do them.

5. Make the goal detailed, specific, and measurable.

6. Fix a time limit as to exactly on what date the goal will be accomplished.

7. Delegate responsibility. Solicit the help of others.

8. Establish checkpoints. See if you're on course and on schedule.

Now that you've completed this "quickie" course on goal-setting, you're ready and prepared to begin a more full and richly rewarding life. And what a life it will be!

These eight steps of the goal-setting process are tried and tested. Try it; you have nothing to lose but a fantastic, fun-filled, exciting, motivating, productive life. Goal-setting truly is the key to success, and it will change your life. I know. It's changed mine!

Chapter Twelve

"America — We're Number One!"

How and Why Americans Become Champions

When I think of America,
I see the great waters of the Mississippi,
The valley of Shenandoah,
And New England's fishing boats going to the sea.

I see the Rocky Mountains,
And those called the Catskills,
The Central Parks with their fountains,
And the southern plantation mills.

I see the waters of the Great Lakes
And the fields of the harvest grain,
The loaves of bread the baker makes
And opportunity for wealth and fame.

I see Concord and Lexington
With the patriot's flag unfurled,
And reflect on the battle won
With the shots heard "'round the world."

I see a land where we may speak as we please
And travel where we want to go,
A land where there is much to see
From white beaches to mountain snow.

I see the majestic Grand Canyon,
The waters of Niagara Falls,
And the colors of the setting sun
Reflected by skyscraper walls.

But with all of America's beauty,
That which means most to me
Is the priceless opportunity
To be what I want to be.

Donald L. Saba

The words of this poem mean a great deal to me. And as you continue to read, you too will find the great significance that they play in all of our lives.

We Are Lucky!

In the course of this book, we have extensively discussed what I believe to be the philosophies most important and vital to us if we are to enjoy the "good life." Probably, when you read about these topics before, it never crossed your mind how lucky you are to read these things. You probably never thought twice about why you and I can enjoy these opportunities to better ourselves and become the best we can be. For this reason alone I wrote this concluding chapter. This chapter is the "why you can" part and the "how" part to all of the others. It's about freedom and what it means and does for us.

Freedom is the key ingredient to our being happy and realizing a full and productive life. In fact, freedom is the key to every success! If we are not free to be what we want to be, why should we work on developing a good self-concept? If we have no freedom of choice, why should we set goals? If we are not free, why should we work harder? Why should we try to excel?

You see, freedom is what allows people to achieve. It's the incentive force of life. It's the motivation that makes people want to sacrifice to reach their ultimate capacity as human beings. Look around and you'll agree. The people who are free have been, are, and always will be the conceivers, believers, and achievers of the world. And where do most of these free, high-achieving people live? America!

The United States of America has 6 percent of the population of the world and occupies 7 percent of its land surface. However, we Americans also own approximately 71 percent of the automobiles, 56 percent of the telephones, 50 percent of the radios, 29 percent of the railroads, and 83

197

percent of the televisions — all of this is owned by only 6 percent of the world's population! Americans enjoy the best standard of living of all human beings on earth.

America truly is Number One — the greatest country in the world! But she's not the greatest because of her land or her resources. She's great because of her people — people like our parents and grandparents who understood the importance of freedom and worked hard, sacrificed, and died to preserve it. America is great because people have made her so!

The ideas and actions of people are what determine the outcome of any endeavor. People make the difference because they perpetuate ideas and philosophies. They determine whether any concept continues. They have power to stop it or keep it going.

Learning About Ourselves

If all of this sounds obvious, it is! But I write it as a reminder. You see, the only way we the people can continue to make a positive difference and continue to perpetuate the present ideas of freedom is if we learn why we are the way we are. Where did our freedom come from? Why are we now free? What will the consequences be if we lose our freedom? How do we keep it? Answers to these questions will help us understand what needs to be done to insure our freedom in the decades to come. This knowledge is essential, as Thomas Jefferson wrote: "If a nation expects to be ignorant and free, it expects what never was and never will be." Therefore, let's examine freedom and define its specific importance to life.

According to a report of Freedom House, an organization established for the strengthening of free societies, as of January 1976, only 19.8 percent of the world's population was free. This is a startling figure, because in January of 1975 the figure was 35 percent. This is a 15.2 percent drop in one year! And the frightening part of this is that the majority of this 19.8 percent of the free people in the world live in America. In other words, America stands between freedom and communist slavery. Eighty percent of the world's population is *not* free!

War and Patriotism

We are presently several years beyond 1976, so I wonder what the present percentage is, now that many other countries have been overthrown by pro-Russian communist dictators. Why do I mention all this? Simply because I want you to start realizing your role as a freedom fighter and be proud you're an American. I want you to develop a deep feeling of patriotism and a love for our country.

I interviewed a war veteran who had an enormous impact on me and helped me more clearly understand patriotism. The following is the script of that interview.

War is never good! It's not right! But sometimes it's inevitable and someone has to fight. I was one of those, and I'm proud I did. I'm proud to be an American. I'm proud I was able to represent freedom and serve my country.

We hear a lot about patriotism, but what is it and how do we get it? Webster says to be a patriot means that you love your country; that you love it enough to live and die for it.

A lot of people look down on war. And everyone should! They say they won't fight and kill, and they have every right to. War is evil and stupid! And as I talk, please understand that I'm not promoting it. We shouldn't have to fight and kill and give our lives to war. But sometimes we have to. Certain "sick" leaders in certain countries give us no choice in the matter. For this reason, let's look at this issue and try to understand the reasons behind fighting.

I guarantee, if some big guy started to boss you around, told you what you had to do, abused your property, and fooled around with your girlfriend or mom — you'd get upset! In fact, I bet most of you would fight! And you wouldn't be fighting just to be fighting. You'd be sticking up for truth, sticking up for what's right.

An army sergeant friend of mine who was in charge of many troops stationed at a fire base camp during the Vietnam war told me there was no such thing as a "conscientious objector," no such thing as a guy who wouldn't fight. While he was there, he had four medics, one for each platoon, who came to his camp claiming to be "conscientious objectors." They put the little red cross on their helmets, indicating they were medical men, and didn't carry guns. This was supposed to protect them, but the enemy didn't care! They shot at them anyway. Do you know what happened to these four "conscientious objector" medics? Before the war was over all four of them were not only carrying weapons, but they were also shooting back! They were saying, "Hey, these cats are trying to kill me and I've got to protect myself," and were asking the sergeant for guns and shooting lessons.

What it boils down to is if we are to be free, we are going to have to fight for it if needs be! Some people want to be free and enjoy all their freedoms of religion or whatever, but they don't feel responsible for sacrificing, fighting, and maybe even dying to preserve this freedom. They expect everyone else to do the work so they can reap the benefits. How inconsiderate and irresponsible! We're either in this American dream of freedom and equality of responsibility all together, or we're not.

We've got people in America who say, "I don't want to go into the service, I don't want to fight, I don't want to register for the draft." But they also say, "I want to be free!" Now, is this right? In essence, what they're saying is, "I don't want to shoot anyone, but I want you to do it for me." Hey, don't be like this! It's not right! Learn to fight your own battles!

Another thing that people complain about is our fighting in other countries. They say, "Why don't we mind our own business and stay in America?" I know you're too young to remember Pearl Habor, but I know you've heard about it. Do you know what was happening before and after the attack? No one was signing up for the armed forces before the attack — it was hard to convince men to join the Army. But as soon as America was attacked, the lines grew longer each day in front of the Army recruiters' office. Men couldn't wait to fight for their country and stick up for the cause of freedom.

Now I ask, Is this what has to happen in order for Americans to get patriotic? Do we have to fight a war on our own beaches before we understand the principles of communist aggression and get Americans excited about defending our freedom? I sure hope not! It will be too late then! These "conscientious objectors" changed their minds about the whole thing when it all of a sudden became a personal threat to them. That's when they picked up guns and started playing rough like the other guys. America has to realize this! Our enemies don't care who we are or what we believe. Dealing with them is not the same as dealing with the grouch neighbors next door. These folks are dead serious about having our land and ruling our country, and they're willing to kill us to get it. We need to stop them before they get too close!

I don't know if you realize it or not, but the communist goal is to take over and rule the world. That's nothing to take lightly, but many do. They say, "Ah, don't get so worked up — you're overreacting! The communists will never come! Don't get so excited!" This is exactly what millions of people have said throughout the world — people in countries like

East Germany, Czechoslovakia, Hungary, Poland, Cuba, Korea, Vietnam, El Salvador, and recently, Afghanistan. None of these folks took communism serious, but now they're asking themselves, "Where will communism strike next? Which country will fall this week or month or year?" Look at the history record — it's obvious the communists are serious about this promise to make the world one communist government power!

Why aren't we serious about preserving freedom? America is the last hope of saving the free lands that still exist in the world! I realize it's our responsibility to promote peace, but it's also our responsibility to fight to preserve freedom wherever we have to.

But you ask, "Why, clear across the world?" I answer, "Why not?" What do we then say, "All right, we'll let communism spread just to Canada and South America, and then that's all"? Heavens, no! We stop it now, as soon as possible, wherever and whenever it starts to occur. Otherwise, someday it will be too late!

We don't want to be governed by communists! If communism is so great, if living conditions are so wonderful in communist countries, why do they have to build fences and walls to keep the people in? Barbed wire, mine fields, and machine gun towers are every mile the whole way along the border from northern to southern Europe. This is more than 500 miles! Those walls are not to keep us out. Nobody wants to go there! How many people or families have you ever heard of that wanted to emigrate to a communist country? When you ride the train into West Berlin, Germany, you must pass through communist East Berlin to get there. They have all the windows in the train blocked out so the passengers can't see the tragic conditions of life under communist rule!

Sure, West Germany has its problems; freedom does create challenges. But how many people do you see trying to climb the walls the other way to go to East Berlin and live? There aren't any! I'm telling you, freedom is the most prized possession on earth! And we need to always remember this so we can preserve it. I want to always be an American. I'm proud to be an American! I hope you are, too!

From Vietnam and Russia to America

What is it about America that makes no one want to leave and live elsewhere? What is it about America that causes thousands of people every year to sacrifice all they have just to come here? I want you to meet some who do know.

Hi, I'm Luc Pham, a Vietnamese refugee. I escaped communism and came to America in 1979, just to be free. When I escaped, I didn't even know where I was going. But I didn't care — I just wanted to get away from the communists. In 1975 I was working for the South Vietnamese government as a police captain. The Americans left in March and the communist government took over immediately, arresting all of the South Vietnamese officials and detaining us in a concentration camp. I was taken from my wife and five children thinking I would never see them again, and was sentenced to life in prison. I was tortured as they tried to get information from me. After two years, I escaped by running away through the jungle to Saigon. There I arranged secretly with friends to be reunited with my family and escape to Thailand in a fishing boat. One hundred people were crammed on this tiny boat with only enough room to squat. We were on the ocean for seven days, and many people died. My friend's mother and some children died and had to be thrown overboard so we could continue. Finally we made it to shore and lived in the refugee camp for five months until we finally came to America. Never will I forget the suffering, discouragement, and maddening nights at sea. It was a death that will remain with me forever, as we thank God for our rebirth and our chance to live as human beings in freedom.

Again I remind you of the question, Why do so many risk their lives trying to be free? Let me tell you why, as another friend speaks.

Communist socialism is not great! My name must remain anonymous, but I can tell you I was born and raised in communist Russia, worked as a journalist, escaped, and came to America in 1980. This gives me an advantage over you. You see, now that I live here in America, I can see on both sides of the wall and know what it's really like to live in communist slavery as well as American capitalism. This is why I wanted to talk to you. There are a lot of things I can tell you about communist socialism, but something you might really be interested in are statistics comparing Russia with America.

If America wanted to be like Russia, all we'd have to do is cut back our paychecks by more than 80 percent, move 33 million workers back to the farm, destroy 59 million TV sets, junk nineteen out of twenty automobiles, rip out thirteen out of every fourteen miles of paved highway, knock down 70 percent of our houses, destroy more than two thousand colleges, burn 85 percent of our museums, and rip out nine out of every ten telephones. Then, to top it off, we would have

202

to buy wheat from capitalistic countries to keep us from starving. Despite communist claims to the contrary, there isn't a communist country in the world that can feed itself or be self-sustaining. In fact, communism is so inefficient that some experts predict Russia, the "mother" of communism, would collapse in fifteen years or less if America withdrew her technological and agricultural expertise and support.

Now can you sense how lucky we are to be free and how fortunate we are to live in free America? Life is so good here it's almost unreal! Our society is now so automated and electronic that even schoolwork is easier for us these days. To do our math, we don't have to know how to add, divide, or count. Our little hand calculators do it all! We don't even have to learn to spell — our computer games do that for us, too! Consequently, we've become "easy," "kicked back," and sometimes downright nonchalant about it all. Because we haven't had to think and sacrifice for what we want and need, we haven't yet learned the full meaning of work, commitment to a cause, and loyalty, all of which are by-products of sacrifice. We have become apathetic to current issues in politics and in world affairs. Our generation seems to be saying "live and let live" and seems not to care about crucial situations and critical decisions. We know we're free and for some reason, that's all we care about!

Hopefully, these negativisms I've just listed about our young generation are not all true. In fact, I hope none of them are, or else we're in a "whole heap" of trouble! If what I accuse us of thinking is true, we'll not only one day ruin ourselves and our communities, but we'll also destroy America, lose our freedoms, and eventually lose our land! We need to understand freedom and realize that freedom is not free. It requires a highly disciplined people to make it work.

Freedom Comes from Sacrifice

You see, freedom is not something Americans have been given. It was not just handed in a golden cup. Freedom is not something that can be taken for granted. We must always remember the sacrifice, hard work, commitment, loyalty, and countless lives that have been given in order to obtain it and keep it. Let's reflect on some past citizens who have contributed to giving us our freedom. We owe them a lot!

I want to start introducing these freedom heroes by asking questions and inquiring into some of the unique experiences that tested their commitment to freedom.

First, what was George Washington doing at Valley Forge? Here was a very wealthy, highly respected man, regarded and admired both in the American colonies and throughout Europe, sitting on a horse by a river at midnight, nearly freezing to death in the winter snows with only a handful of half-dead and sick fighting men.

In the most crucial battle of the Revolutionary War, with frostbitten, gallant soldiers who had to wrap rags around their feet for shoes because they had none, Washington went into battle to defy overwhelming odds. Why? With all of the great and luxurious comforts of life to enjoy, why did Washington willingly give them up and sacrifice his life and personal honor to take up arms to fight and die if necessary? Think about it! Would you, as easy-going "comfortable" individuals, be willing to sacrifice all that you have for the cause of freedom?

Second, why was Thomas Jefferson willing to spend all his personal funds to begin the University of Virginia when he could have had a life of luxury and ease? Jefferson died in poverty after fighting his creditors the last twelve years of his life. What motivated him to unselfishly give all he had to better his country?

Third, what happened to the signers of the Declaration of Independence when they put their lives and futures on the dotted line so that you and I could be free? Five signers were captured by the British as traitors and were tortured before they died. Twelve had their homes ransacked and burned. Two lost their sons in the Revolutionary War, and another had two sons captured. Nine of the fifty-six fought and died from wounds or the hardships of the Revolutionary War.

What kind of men were they? Twenty-four were lawyers and jurists. Eleven were merchants and nine were farmers and large plantation owners. They signed the Declaration of Independence knowing full well that the penalty would be death if they were captured. These were not wild, terrorist men. These were wealthy, educated, softspoken family men. They had security, but they valued liberty more. Confidently, they firmly pledged: "For the support of this declaration, with a firm reliance on the protection of the Divine Providence, we mutually pledge to each other our lives, our fortunes, and our sacred honor."

These men sacrificed greatly, but what about the women of the Revolution? I know you've heard of Paul Revere, but did you know there was a female "Paul Revere" who also made a heroic ride? During the war, a sixteen-year-old girl named Sybil Ludington took a midnight ride for the rebel cause that was even more dangerous than the famed ride of Revere.

On the night of April 25, 1777, two thousand British soldiers landed and immediately started to destroy the rebels' supply houses as they proceeded inland from Connecticut. Discovering kegs of rum, they began to indulge, whereupon they got drunk, started shooting their guns, and burned down the town.

That evening, a messenger with a bullet wound in his back rode to the Ludington farm, twenty miles west of Danbury. He alerted Sybil's father, the local commander of the militia, to the danger in Danbury.

Colonel Ludington didn't know what to do. If he left to notify his four hundred volunteers, he would not make it back in time to lead them in battle.

Sybil offered to go in his place. Riding sidesaddle, she rode forty miles — twenty-six miles further than Paul Revere — through a dangerous, hostile, Indian-infested region stretching between the British and American lines.

As she rode, she shouted the warning, banging loudly on the doors with a big stick as she passed by.

Just as the sun was beginning to rise, Sybil Ludington arrived home, an exhausted heroine. Because of her, American rebels won the battle.

An American Patriot in Korea

These sacrifices and commitments for freedom happened two hundred years ago. Have any happened lately? I want you to meet a close friend of mine who tells a story about a modern-day hero who was willing to sacrifice all that he had for the cause of freedom.

My name is Larry Steed. I spent twenty years in the Air Force as a fighter pilot. During my life I have been privileged to defend this country, and I have observed the sacrifices of many of my fellow countrymen. *Duty, honor, sacrifice,* and *integrity* are all great and meaningful words. Let me tell you the story of a man I met — a man who put all these words into action. This man, I'll call him Bill, was a marine jet fighter pilot during the Korean War. Bill was flying a tough mission when his aircraft was hit by a large caliber shell from an anti-aircraft gun. Moments later he found himself hanging from his parachute, about to land somewhere in enemy territory. It seemed that he no sooner hit the ground when he was surrounded by a large group of North Korean soldiers pointing guns and bayonets at him. They immediately started taking his equipment, including his coat, watch, boots, and flying suit. This left him standing in a snow-covered field in only his socks and underwear.

Then an enemy truck pulled up, Bill was ordered into the back, and he started a long, freezing ride north to a prisoner-of-war camp. The truck ride lasted all that day and through the night. He thought about escape but knew he could not survive the cold with no coat or boots, and even if he did survive the elements, a tall, blond American running around in his underwear has a way of standing out in a country populated by Orientals!

As he arrived at the gates of the gates of the prison camp, Bill was thinking he would at last have a chance to get warm and put on some clothing. Instead, he was forced into a small room with no heat and placed on a small wooden stool. There he came face to face with Captain Chea, the camp interrogator, a man he would come to know very well. It was Captain Chea's job to find out all the useful military information he could from each prisoner. As Chea sized up Bill he decided to play the "good-guy" role. He offered Bill a cigarette, but Bill declined. He asked where Bill was from and received Bill's name, rank, and serial number in reply — all that is required by the Geneva Convention for prisoners of war. He asked what kind of plane Bill flew — same answer — name, rank, and serial number. The questions continued for several more minutes when finally, and without warning, Chea turned and knocked Bill off the stool with a vicious blow to the head. Before he could recover, Bill was grabbed from behind, and Chea hit and kicked him into consciousness.

When Bill came to, he found himself alone in a tiny one-man cell that he would soon learn the other prisoners called the hooch. It was cold. He was hungry. His body ached all over, but most of all he felt scared and alone.

As he sat there gathering his thoughts, the door flew open and he was dragged back to the interrogation room. And there waiting was Captain Chea. Chea explained that he knew the Americans had been using germ warfare against the North Koreans and that all Bill had to do was sign a simple statement acknowledging this and he would be fed, given warm clothing, and assigned a warm, comfortable room with some other prisoners. Chea's reward for this eloquent little speech was Bill's name, rank, and serial number.

At this, Chea flew into a rage. Bill was tied to a chair with his hands tied behind him. The chair was tipped back, a towel was placed over Bill's face, and a bucket of water was poured on the towel. Each time Bill tried to breathe, more water was poured. It was just like drowning. Bill struggled to get some air, but there was only water. Soon he went limp and passed out, near death.

When he came to, he was again asked the questions and told to sign the paper. Bill sounded like a stuck record — name, rank, and serial number. His hands were still tied behind his back. Suddenly someone forced a round stick the size of a broom handle with a dirty rag wrapped around it into his mouth like a bit on a horse. He felt a knee on the back of his head. Then someone pulled. As the pressure increased, so did the pain. Bill felt his jaw dislocate. His muffled scream was interrupted only when his eardrum ruptured. What followed was more like a nightmare than reality. He was aware only of pain, cold, and darkness.

When he next awoke, he found himself alone in the hooch once more. Pain racked his body. Hunger attacked his stomach, and for the first time he wondered if he could endure another torture session. It was impossible to tell what time or day it was. For what seemed like days he laid there until the door flung open. Once again he was grabbed and dragged to the waiting room and Captain Chea. As he entered the room he saw a bowl of hot rice and some cooked vegetables and hot tea. Also on the table was the germ warfare paper and a pen. Chea told Bill he could eat as soon as he signed the paper.

In some ways, this was worse than the physical torture. Bill knew he was weak from hunger and must have food to survive. But at the same time, he knew he had never been involved in germ warfare and that the communists would use these signed documents to spread their lies around the world. Bill reasoned that he had always been prepared to die for his country each time he climbed into his airplane. The death he now faced would be long and agonizing, but nevertheless he was willing to risk it and not compromise all that he stood for.

As weak as he was, Bill was able to generate enough power to reach out and kick over the table with the food and paper. He then looked into Chea's startled face and mumbled his name, rank, and serial number. A rifle butt hit him from behind, and the blow was quick and merciful.

Later, as soon as he could sit up, he was fed broth that was flavored with tiny pieces of pumpkin and pig fat. Little did Bill know that this and rice was to become his main diet for the next two years.

After a few days, except for the severe pain in his ear and jaw, Bill was starting to think he would be okay. Then the guards came and took him back to see Chea. Chea explained that he was given these few days to rest as an example of the great mercy and humanity of the North Korean people. But now it was time to face the fact that Bill was a war criminal and that he must confess his involvement with germ warfare. Bill did not respond, so out came the chair, towel, and buckets of water.

Bill regained consciousness back in the hooch. This went on every day for a week. Many other painful tortures were used, but Bill would not yield. Then one day the guard took Bill from the hooch and marched him to the center of the camp. He was handed a shovel and told to dig his grave. Even though the ground was frozen hard and Bill was very weak from his diet of broth and pig fat, he was finally able to dig a grave about two feet deep when Chea showed up.

Chea handed him the germ warfare paper and a pen and told him to sign or he would be shot then and there. Bill looked at the form, looked at Chea, and tore the paper in half. Chea whipped out his Russian pistol and ordered Bill into the grave. He placed the cold steel barrel of that gun against Bill's temple and pulled the trigger. It was the loudest click Bill had ever heard. And for what seemed like an eternity, Bill didn't breathe. Just as he realized he hadn't been shot, a rifle butt smashed against the back of his head again and everything went black.

When Bill awoke it was night, and he was half-frozen from the cold. He crawled out of his grave and made his way to the hooch. In the next six months he went through this routine more times than he could remember. Sometimes the gun would be empty and other times it would be held just over the top of his head and fired. Each time he was knocked to the ground with a rifle butt.

Bill became a symbol of determination to the other prisoners, and about all Chea heard from anyone was a lot of names, ranks, and serial numbers. Finally the peace talks were concluded and prisoners were being placed in trucks to be taken south to their own people. No one ever seemed to come for Bill. The last truck pulled into the camp and the twenty-five remaining prisoners were placed in the back. Bill was taken to the small two-story building next to where the last truck was parked. He was pushed into an upstairs room whose window overlooked the truck below. In that room sat Chea. He said, "Look out the window and see your friends below. I offer you a choice. You sign this document and confess your involvement with germ warfare, in which case you can go downstairs and get on that truck. Or, if you don't, I'll give a signal and that truck will leave and no one will ever hear of you again." Bill looked out the window at his friends who were waving for him to come and join them in the truck — the truck that would take him to his friends, his country, his wife and children — everything he held dear. Then he looked at the document. It was just a piece of paper. Surely, everyone would know that if he signed it, it would be just so that he could go home! They would understand all the pain, torture, and misery that he had gone through. Who could blame him for signing this lousy piece of paper? This was the moment of truth. He looked again at the truck, picked up the pen, read the form over for the last time, looked Chea in the eye, and told him to "Shove it!"

Bill was eventually released, and he told me his story several years later.

Would You Fight to Preserve Freedom?

How many of you would be willing to give this much for America and the cause of freedom? Think about it! Over 650,000 Americans have already died in battle. From the grassy fields of Lexington to the rice paddies of Vietnam, thousands of lives have been sacrificed. And why did they die? They died for the cause of freedom! They gave their lives so that you and I, as well as people from many other countries that are not strong enough by themselves, can be free. These brave men and women understood that democracy is the system that allows people to be champions. They knew it must be preserved and felt that it was worth fighting for.

When evil men with evil philosophies tried to take away these freedoms and opportunities for success and happiness, *someone* had to stick up for what was right. *Someone* had to stick up for man's inalienable rights. *Someone* had to fight to preserve freedom! And these gallant Americans stepped forth and were willing to do it. They knew freedom was the most prized possession on earth, and they died for it. All of them chose the freedom to enjoy life, liberty, and the pursuit of happiness, even at the cost of their lives. They decided they would rather die to preserve freedom for future generations than exist without freedom. The "Credo of Thomas Tebbs" explains their philosophy.

Credo of Thomas Tebbs

I do not choose to be a common man. It is my right to be uncommon if I can. I seek opportunity, not security. I do not wish to be a kept citizen, humbled and dulled by having the state look after me. I want to take the calculated risk, to dream and to build, to fail and succeed. I refuse to barter incentive for a dole. I prefer the challenge of life to the guaranteed existence, the thrill of fulfillment to the state of calm utopia. I will not trade freedom for beneficence, nor dignity for a handout. It is my heritage to think and act for myself, enjoy the benefit of my creations, and to face the world boldly and say, this I have done.

Has the time passed when we no longer have to make these choices? Should we, the young people of America, settle back and be content as common men? Is all the hard work and sacrificing finished so we don't have to do it any more?

I'm telling you, No! Now it's *our* turn to sacrifice for America! It's now *our* turn to preserve our freedoms for future generations! Freedom is not a destination — it didn't come overnight. Freedom is a journey; a constant struggle; a hard-hitting battle against strong forces of opposing philosophies. And, most importantly, freedom continues from generation to generation only if those who enjoy it continue to make it work.

I'm sure you agree that you like being free. You enjoy living in a free country with all of these luxuries, benefits, and freedoms.

Freedom Is in Danger

But these freedoms are in danger! I don't want you to think I'm claiming there's a communist behind every tree, but the threat of losing our freedom is there. The communists are clever and real! They don't want to attack America. It didn't work for Japan, and the communists don't want to risk losing that kind of confrontation. They simply plan to propagandize and slowly change America's thinking from the inside.

I'm sure you've all experienced what I call the "Hot Tub Theory." When you injure an ankle, you're supposed to put it in freezing cold water to immediately stop the swelling. What happens to you when you do this?

First of all, your heart seems to stop, and then you get pains in your leg and neck, then you lose your breath, get a severe headache, and take your foot out quickly. All of this happens in the space of maybe three seconds and oh, baby, does it hurt! No way will you put your foot back in that ice water!

In another instance you've been injured for a while and this time the treatment is to get into a hot tub (115° hot!) all the way up to your chin. To this you think, Great, this will be relaxing. But no sooner has your body been immersed than you come flying out of the scalding water. It's way too hot for you!

Both cases are interesting and are crucial to the "Hot Tub Theory." In fact, they both prove the theory true!

The theory is that you can't bear any extreme temperature all at once. But if you were to get into lukewarm water, get used to it, and then add ice or heat little by little until you reached the desired temperature, you wouldn't feel the shock or notice the temperature change, and you wouldn't mind staying in there indefinitely. Eventually you would freeze to death or fry!

This is exactly how the communists plan to take over the free world; how Americans will be killed; how American philosophies and the free enterprise capitalistic system will eventually die. The "commies" will filter in low-key, stir up unrest in America, subtly propagandize, and slowly turn on the "cold" or "hot" until we're used to it and "can't see the forest from the trees." Think about this as you read about the reasons why we don't ever want to be ruled by the communists.

A Polish Girl, Communism, and Democracy

In Poland, a relatively new communist country, the situation is brutal! I interviewed a beautiful young woman who, because of security reasons, asked to remain anonymous. In our lengthy conversation, she really opened my eyes to the communist world and its philosophies and enforced behavior patterns. She explained why so many of the people in communist countries who have not yet been brainwashed want to get out. I asked her how she was able to escape. Her story is not typical, because she made it. Obviously, she didn't try to climb the wall or rush the barbed wire fence. If she or anyone else tries this, they are shot on sight. More than seventy people have tried this to date, and none are alive to tell about it.

You see, in communist countries people are forced to live in a Godless society with no moral values of honesty, integrity, truthworthiness, or virtue. The communist leaders have no value for human life. They believe a person is just a number, an expendable number that can easily be done away with and replaced. With this understanding, is it any wonder why people want to escape but are afraid to attempt it?

This young Polish girl wanted so badly to leave Poland that she decided to apply for permission. She went to the government, and they told her she must get permission from her employer. So she asked her employer for a leave of absence without pay, but he wouldn't give it to her. Finally, when everything she tried had failed, her boss, who was an official in the Communist Party, took her aside and told her how to cheat to get out. He told her to just apply for her usual number of days of annual leave, and she would have no problem getting it. This way she could get a passport.

Yes, communism is this regimented. Every person in a communist country has to carry an identification card with them at all times. This card includes a photo, fingerprints, and address. If a person moves, he must report the address change to the police station within three days. This makes it easy for the communists to follow anyone anywhere, anytime. They constantly monitor every move you make and everything you say. If you try to cross them, they put you in prison or kill you.

Well, because the Polish girl wasn't in trouble and was considered a committed communist, she received her passport. As she left Poland, she was allowed to exchange her money for the American equivalent of only about ten dollars. This was to prevent her from staying away and spending Polish money in another country. Her holiday pass was to go to England for a few days and then return.

She didn't return. She stayed in England for six months, emigrated to Canada, and finally got to the land of dreams — America. If the Polish Communist government had even thought for a minute that she was going to leave for good, they never would have let her go. This is hard for us to imagine because we can come and go as we please. What a difference between communism and democracy!

Education is another topic I discussed with her during our interview. It is of utmost importance to the communists. School is mandatory until age eighteen. There is no freedom of choice — you must attend all classes and never sluff. And you must take specified subjects. For instance, at age seven, communist children in Warsaw Pact countries must all take Russian. It's compulsory from then until age sixteen, and if you're lucky enough to go to college you must study it there, too! Students are taught that one day soon, Russian will be the language spoken in every country of the world.

Military service is also mandatory. Every boy must put in a minimum of two years of extensive military training before he is out of school. Girls are required to enlist for one year.

The Polish girl went on to explain to me that there is absolutely no drug problem in communist countries. And do you know why? The main reason is that young communists are totally disciplined and dedicated, and they are taught that drugs are harmful to their bodies and will detract from their ultimate potential.

Wow! This is so logical! Why can't America's youth understand this and do what's right? Why aren't we smart enough to stop doing something if it's so harmful and bad?

Communists Are "Committed"

In communist countries children have it "pounded into them" that sacrifice and life for country come above all else. And the startling results the communists are getting should make us worry! This Polish girl told me a story about her Russian girlfriend. The Russian girl expressed

213

to her that she felt very guilty about living in Poland. The reason for her guilt was that she was living in relatively comfortable circumstances in Poland while her Russian people were back home working very hard to build socialism and communism. She said she was miserable among all the Polish luxuries (which by American standards are still poverty), and if Russia asked her to leave her husband and her young child and go back and work in Siberia for the good of her people, she would do it! And you know, she's not the only one! Millions and millions of communists are committed to do whatever is asked of them for the betterment and cause of communism. What dedication! What powerful devotion! They definitely are champions of communism!

Now I ask, where are the champions of our capitalism? Do we as Americans have this same patriotic commitment to our country? Do we wholeheartedly believe in our cause of capitalism?

Communist youth don't take drugs and are totally committed and dedicated to the idea of total sacrifice for their country, stated my Polish friend. They completely understand communist law, doctrine, and principles, and they practice them stoutheartedly every day of their lives. They firmly believe that communism is the best and only workable system in the world.

"On the other hand," she observed, "some of America's young people do take drugs and abuse their bodies, and it makes them mentally and physically unfit for anything." She also noticed, through her experience in America's school system as a teacher, that many young Americans don't have the slightest clue about capitalism or free enterprise. Young Americans don't understand why our system truly is the best in the world and why it's worth preserving. She then asked me, "How can young Americans be committed to a cause they really know nothing about?"

Americans Need More Commitment

Therefore, if you look at the devotion and commitment of communists and then compare it to some young Americans who are just wandering around getting stoned, avoiding the draft, sluffing school, and complaining about our government that they don't even understand, what would you conclude? If we ever had to fight a battle, whose side would you want to be on? Hey, I want to be on America's side, too, but I don't want to lose! We had better change our ways! I realize most of our soldiers and the majority of young people in the USA aren't as bad as she's described, but even if a few are, it's too many! We have got to commit ourselves to becoming the best we can be and learn about our great system so we can become dedicated and committed to preserving it. We need to cultivate the same degree of willingness to sacrifice for our country and the same intensity of devotion to our free enterprise system that communist youth have for theirs.

The way we make this change and develop this new devotion is through education and awareness. By knowing what's wrong, we can change it and do what's right.

For example, one important area we need to clean up is our court system. Our criminal justice system is inadequate. In fact, it's a joke! In a page of the *Wall Street Journal*, United Technologies Corporation ran the following message:

> There's a major crime committed in America at the rate of one every 3 seconds. A murder every 24 minutes. A robbery every 68 seconds. An assault every 51 seconds. A burglary every 10 seconds. A theft every 5 seconds. The odds are narrowing that you will be a victim of a bodily or property assault. But the person who commits a crime has only a 1 in 5 chance of being arrested, and a 1 in 100 chance of going to jail.
>
> In other words, those who break the law are kept off the hook and continue to break the law. Our justice system is supposed to be "just" for all — not merely "just" for the accused! We need to do something about this for our protection!

These statistics are alarming, but I believe another area we need to clean up, which is one of the causes of the above statistics, is the worst and most tragic of all. The flag, Pledge of Allegiance, free enterprise, and the American Success Dream — these symbols and philosophies, which have made America great, are misunderstood and ridiculed by youth today.

215

Recently I interviewed 100 high school students. Of them, only 68 knew all the words to the "Star-Spangled Banner"; 86 knew the Pledge of Allegiance; 43 knew what the different parts of the flag stood for; and only 5 could give any advantages the free enterprise system has over communism. This is pathetic! Why are we like this? Why have Americans fallen short of the previous Number One mark?

One reason is that we've lost some of our pride in "made in America," and we don't take as much responsibility for our actions as we used to. For example, in 1973, Ford Motor Company lost a record 93 million dollars. That same year, Mercedes Benz had its best profit year in its history. What made the difference? The difference boils down to pride in personal workmanship. Unlike Ford cars, Mercedes cars are hand-crafted by workers who believe pay equals productivity. When each worker finishes his part of a car, he takes full responsibility for his work and signs his name to a sticker which is visible on the car. Mercedes cars are great because the company and its employees take a great deal of pride in themselves, the reputation of their company, and the product they make.

We used to be like this and in fact at one time not long ago, we had so much pride as Americans that we led the world in every field. Can we do it again? Can we rekindle and recapture that commitment, the love of an honest day's work, and the proud fighting heart we Americans once had?

Live, Not Die, for America

You bet we can! In fact, we young Americans are already doing it! The tide of pride is turning! Our generation is once again believing and emulating the words of our forefathers and past patriots. We have once again committed to their cause of freedom which is now our cause.

Patrick Henry shook his fist at King George III and proclaimed, "Is life so dear or peace so sweet as to be purchased at the price of chains or slavery? Forbid it, Almighty God! I know not what course others may take, but as for me, give me liberty or give me death!"

The early American naval hero, John Paul Jones, who,

with his back to the wall, his guns out of order, and his ships being sunk all around him, rose to the occasion and answered the call from the English navy to surrender, "I have not yet begun to fight!"

Abraham Lincoln summed up our American patriotic feeling and our commitment to making our free system endure throughout all generations:

> Let reverence for the laws of liberty be breathed by every American mother to the lisping babe that prattles on her lap — let it be taught in schools, in seminaries, and in colleges — let it be preached from the pulpit, proclaimed in legislative halls, and enforced in courts of justice.
>
> In short, let liberty become the political religion of the nation; and let the old and the young, the rich and the poor, the grave and the happy, of all sexes and tongues and colors and conditions, sacrifice unceasingly upon its altars.

We need to cherish liberty! We need to perpetuate liberty! We need to be proud we are free Americans!

Thoughout this chapter I have written extensively about being willing to die for liberty and America. And sure, it's great to be willing to die for a cause. But don't you think it would be better to *live* for it? We, as young Americans, need to get involved in community meetings and state-wide political functions. We need to take an active role in current issues and laws that effect our lifestyle. We need to learn about candidates who run for office and what they stand for. If we want to change things or keep them as they are, we need to actively support programs and individuals who share our beliefs. This means not just verbal support, but when you reach voting age, you actually vote to support them! Your vote, just one, single, solitary, individual vote, could make the difference! For instance:

In 1645 — *one vote* gave Oliver Cromwell control of England.

In 1649 — *one vote* caused Charles I of England to be executed.

In 1776 — *one vote* gave America the English language instead of German.

In 1839 — *one vote* elected Marcus Morton governor of Massachusetts.

In 1845 — *one vote* brought Texas into the Union.

In 1868 — *one vote* saved President Andrew Johnson from impeachment.

In 1876 — *one vote* gave Rutherford D. Hayes the presidency of the United States.

In 1923 — *one vote* gave Adolph Hitler leadership of the Nazi party.

See what I mean? You — yes, you, little old you, are important, and you need to get involved. Remember, America is the greatest country in the world because of her people — because our fathers and forefathers got involved. Now *you* have that same opportunity. President Reagan reminds us:

> America was founded on a dream, and now it's your turn to keep that dream moving. We've always reached for a new spirit and aimed at a higher goal. We've always been courageous, determined, unafraid, and bold. Who among us ever wants to say we no longer have those qualities?
>
> We look to you to meet the great challenge, to reach beyond the commonplace and not fall short for lack of creativity and courage. And to do this? All you need to begin with is a dream to do better than ever before. All you need to have is faith and that dream will come true. All you need to do is act — and the time for action is *now*.

Get high, take yourself off the shelf, realize you were born to succeed, deal with your problems, always "do it," discover who you are, reach for success through academic achievement, avoid drugs, recondition your thinking, set goals, take pride in yourself, and learn about our fabulous free enterprise system.

Always strive to become better today than you were yesterday and decide to become a champion. A champion in effort! A champion in life! A champion for America! Remember, you were born to succeed and the best is yet to be. Get high and go for it!

THE END
(which is the beginning)

Notes

Notes

Notes

Notes

Notes

Notes